I0422994

Böhm-Bawerk's Criticism of Marx by Rudolf Hilferding
First Prism Key Press Edition 2011

Prism Key Press
New York, NY 10001
PrismKeyPress.com

ISBN-13: 978-1467902823

Böhm-Bawerk's Criticism of Marx

Rudolf Hilferding

Contents

Preface

THE publication of the third volume of *Capital* has made hardly any impression upon bourgeois economic science. We have seen nothing of the "jubilant hue and cry" anticipated by Sombart. [1] No struggle of intellects has taken place; there was no contest *in majorem scientiae gloriam*. For in the theoretical field bourgeois economics no longer engages in blithe and joyous fights. As spokesman for the bourgeoisie, it enters the lists only where the bourgeoisie has practical interests to defend. In the economico-political struggles of the day it faithfully reflects the conflict of interests of the dominant cliques, but it shuns the attempt to consider the totality of social relationships, for it rightly feels that any such consideration would be incompatible with its continued existence as bourgeois economics. Even where the bourgeois economists, compiling their "systems" or writing their "sketches," must perforce speak of the relationships of the whole, the only whole they succeed in presenting is laboriously pieced together out of its separate parts. They have ceased to deal with principles; they have ceased to be systematic; they have become eclectics and syncretists. Dietzel, author of *Theoretische Sozialökonomie,* is perfectly logical when, making the best of a bad business, he raises eclecticism to the rank of a principle.

The only exception is the psychological school of political economy. The adherents of this school resemble the classical economists and the Marxists in that they endeavor to apprehend economic phenomena from a unitary outlook. Opposing Marxism with a circumscribed theory, their criticism is systematic in character, and their critical attitude is forced upon them because they have started from totally different premises. As early as 1884, in his *Capital and Interest,* Böhm-Bawerk joined issue with the first volume of *Capital,* and soon after the publication of the third volume of that work he issued a detailed criticism the substance of which was reproduced in the second edition of his Capital and Interest [German edition 1900]. [2] He believes he has proved the untenability of economic Marxism, and confidently announces that "the beginning of the end of the labor theory of value" has been inaugurated by the publication of the third volume of *Capital.*

Since his criticism deals with principles, since he does not attack isolated and arbitrarily selected points or conclusions, but questions and reflects as untenable the very foundation of the Marxist system, possibility is afforded for a fruitful discussion. But since the Marxist system has to be dealt with in its entirety, this discussion must be more detailed than that which is requisite to meet the objections of the eclectics, objections based upon misunderstanding and concerned only with individual details.

Footnotes

1. Werner Sombart,"Zur Kritik des ökonomischen Systems von Karl Marx," *Archiv für Soziale Gesetzgebung und Statistik,* Vol. VII (1894), pp. 555-594.

2. All Hilferding's subsequent references to this book are from the second German edition (1900), and it is therefore impossible for us to refer the reader to Smart's English translation, made from the first German edition (1884). A third German edition was published in 1914. [Translators]

Chapter I
Value as an Economic Category

THE analysis of the commodity constitutes the starting point of the Marxist system. Böhm-Bawerk's criticism is primarily leveled against this analysis.

Böhm-Bawerk contends that Marx fails to adduce either an empirical or a psychological proof of his thesis that the principle of value is to be sought in labor. He "prefers another, and for such a subject somewhat singular line of evidence–the method of a purely logical proof, a dialectic deduction from the very nature of exchange." [1]

Marx had found in Aristotle the idea that exchange cannot exist without equality, and equality cannot exist without commensurability. Starting with this idea, he conceives the exchange of two commodities under the form of an equation, and from this infers that a common factor of the same amount must exist in the things exchanged and thereby equated, and then proceeds to search for this common factor to which the two equated things must, as exchange values, be reducible. Now according to Böhm-Bawerk the most vulnerable point in the Marxist theory is to be found in the logical and systematic processes of distillation by means of which Marx obtains the sought-for "common factor" in labor. They exhibit, he declares, almost as many cardinal errors as there are points in the argument. From the beginning Marx only puts into the sieve those exchangeable [should read, "interchangeable," R. H.] things which he desires finally to winnow out as "the common factor," and he leaves all the others outside. That is to say, he limits from the outset the field of his search to "commodities," considering these solely as the products of labor contrasted with the gifts of nature. Now it stands to reason, continues Böhm-Bawerk, that if exchange really means an equalization, which assumes the existence of "a common factor of the same amount," this common factor must be sought and found in every species of goods which is brought into exchange, not only in products of labor, but also in gifts of nature, such as the soil, wood in trees, water power, etc. To exclude these exchangeable goods is a gross error of method, and the exclusion of the gifts of nature is the less to be justified because many natural gifts, such as the soil, are among the most important objects of property and commerce, and also because it is impossible to affirm that in nature's gifts exchange values [this of course should be "prices"! R. H.] are always established arbitrarily and by accident. Marx is likewise careful to avoid mentioning that he excludes from investigation a part of exchangeable goods. In this case, as in so many others, he manages to glide with eel-like dialectic skill over the difficult points of his argument. He omits to call his readers' attention to the fact that his idea of "commodities" is narrower than that of exchangeable goods as a whole. Nay, more, he continually endeavors to obliterate the distinction. He is compelled to take this course, for unless Marx had confined his research, at the decisive point, to products of labor, if he had sought for the common factor in the "exchangeable" gifts of nature as well, it would have become obvious that labor cannot be the common factor. Had he carried out this limitation quite clearly and openly, the gross fallacy of method would inevitably have struck both himself and his readers. The trick could only have been performed, as Marx performed it, with the aid of the marvelous dialectic skill wherewith he glides swiftly and lightly over the knotty point.

But by means of the artifice just described, proceeds our critic, Marx has merely succeeded in convincing us that labor can in fact enter into the competition. The exclusion of other competitors is effected by two arguments, each of a few words only, but each containing a very serious logical fallacy. In the first of these Marx excludes all "geometrical, physical, chemical, or other natural qualities of the commodities," for "their physical qualities claim our attention only in so far as they affect the utility of the commodities–make them use values. On the other hand, the exchange relation of commodities is evidently characterized by the abstraction of their use values," because "within this relation (the exchange relation) one use value is as good as another provided only it be present in the proper proportion."

Here, says Böhm-Bawerk, Marx falls into a grave error. He confuses the disregarding of a genus with the disregarding of the specific forms in which this genus manifests itself. The special forms under which use value may appear may be disregarded, but the use value of the commodity in general must never be disregarded. Marx might have seen that we do not absolutely disregard use value, from the fact that there can be no exchange value where there is not a use value–a fact which Marx himself is repeatedly forced to admit.

Let us for a moment interrupt our recapitulation of Böhm-Bawerk's criticism by a brief interpolation calculated to throw light upon the psychology no less than upon the logic of the leader of the psychological school.

When I disregard the "specific forms in which use value may manifest itself," disregarding, therefore, use value in its concreteness, I have, as far as I am concerned, disregarded use value in general, since, as far as I am concerned, use value exists in its concreteness solely as a thus or thus constituted use value. Having ceased for me to be a use value, it matters nothing to me that it has a use value for others, possesses utility for this or that other person. I do not exchange it until the moment arrives when it has ceased to possess a use value for me. This applies literally to the production of commodities in its developed form. Here the individual produces commodities of but one kind, commodities of which one specimen at most can possess a use value for him, whereas in the mass the commodities have for him no such use value. It is a precondition to the exchangeability of the commodities that they should possess utility for others, but since for me they are

11

devoid of utility, the use value of my commodities is in no sense a measure even for my individual estimate of value, and still less is it a measure of an objective estimate of value. It avails nothing to say that the use value consists of the capacity of these commodities to be exchanged for other commodities, for this would imply that the extent of the "use value" is now determined by the extent of the exchange value, not the extent of the exchange value by the extent of the use value.

As long as goods are not produced for the purpose of exchange, are not produced as commodities, as long, that is to say, as exchange is no more than an occasional incident wherein superfluities only are exchanged, goods confront one another solely as use values.

"The proportions in which they are exchangeable are at first quite a matter of chance. What makes them exchangeable is the mutual desire of their owners to alienate them. Meantime the need for foreign objects of utility gradually establishes itself. The constant repetition of exchange makes it a normal social act. In the course of time, therefore, some portion at least of the products of labor must be produced with a special view to exchange. From that moment the distinction becomes firmly established between the utility of an object for the purposes of consumption, and its utility for the purposes of exchange. Its use value becomes distinguished from its exchange value. On the other hand, the quantitative proportion in which the articles are exchangeable becomes dependent on their production itself. Custom stamps them as values with definite magnitudes." [2]

We have in fact nothing more than a disregard by Marx of the specific forms in which the use value manifests itself. For the use value remains the "bearer of value." This is indeed self-evident, for "value" is nothing more than an economic modification of use value. It is solely the anarchy of the contemporary method of production, owing to which under certain conditions (a glut) a use value becomes a non-use-value and consequently valueless, which makes the recognition of this self-evident truth a matter of considerable importance.

Let us return to Böhm-Bawerk. The second step in the argument, he tells us, is still worse. Marx contends that if the use value of commodities be disregarded, there remains in them but one other quality, that of being products of labor. But do there not remain a number of other qualities? Such is Böhm-Bawerk's indignant inquiry. Have they not the common quality of being scarce in proportion to demand? Is it not common to them to be the objects of demand and supply, or that they are appropriated, or that they are natural products? Is it not common to them that they cause expense to their producers–a quality to which Marx draws attention in the third volume of *Capital?* Why should not the principle of value reside in any one of these qualities as well as in the quality of being products of labor? For in support of this latter proposition Marx has not adduced a shred of positive evidence. His sole argument is the negative one, that the use value, thus happily disregarded and out of the way, is not the principle of exchange value. But does not this negative argument apply with equal force to all the other common qualities overlooked [!] by Marx? This is not all. Marx writes as follows: "Along with the useful qualities of the products [of labor] we put out of sight both the useful character of the various kinds of labor embodied in them, and the concrete forms of that labor; there is nothing left but what is common to them all; they are reduced to one and the same sort of labor, human labor in the abstract." [3] But in saying this he admits that for an exchange relationship, not only one use value but also any one kind of labor "is just as good as another, provided only it be present in the proper proportion." It follows that the identical evidence on which Marx formulated his verdict of exclusion in the case of use value will hold good as regards labor. Labor and use value, says Böhm-Bawerk, have a qualitative side and a quantitative side. Just as the use value differs according as it is manifested in a table or in yarn, so also does labor differ as carpentry or spinning. And just as we may compare different kinds of labor according to their quantity, so

13

we may compare use values of different kinds according to the varying amount of use value. It is quite impossible to understand why the very same evidence should result in the exclusion of one competitor and in the assigning of the prize to the other. Marx might just as well have reversed his reasoning process and have disregarded labor.

Such is Marx's logic, such his method of procedure, as reflected in the mind of Böhm-Bawerk. His procedure, according to the latter, was perfectly arbitrary. Although in an utterly unjustified but extremely artful manner he has managed to secure that nothing but the products of labor shall be left to be exchanged, it was impossible for him to adduce even the slightest ground for the contention that the common quality which must presumably be present in the commodities to be exchanged is to be sought and found in labor. Only by willfully ignoring a number of other qualities, only by his utterly unwarranted disregard of use value, did Marx attain the desired result. Just as little as the classical economists was Marx in a position to furnish an atom of proof on behalf of the proposition that labor is the principle of value.

Böhm-Bawerk's critical question to which Marx is alleged to have given so fallacious an answer is the question: what right had Marx to proclaim labor to be the sole creator of value? Our counter-criticism must in the first instance consist of a demonstration that the analysis of the commodity furnishes the desired answer.

To Böhm-Bawerk, the Marxist analysis establishes a contrast between utility and the product of labor. Now we fully agree with Böhm-Bawerk that no such contrast exists. Labor must be done on most things in order to render them useful. On the other hand, when we estimate the utility of a thing, it is a matter of indifference to us how much labor has been expended on it. A good does not become a commodity merely in virtue of being the product of labor. But only in so far as it is a *commodity* does a good exhibit the contrasted qualities of use value and value. Now a good becomes a commodity solely through entering into a relationship with other goods, a relationship which becomes manifest in the act of exchange, and which, quantitatively regarded, appears as the exchange value of the good. The quality of functioning as an exchange value thus determines the commodity character of the good. But a commodity cannot of its own initiative enter into relationships with other commodities; the material relationship between commodities is of necessity the expression of a personal relationship between their respective owners. As owners of commodities, these reciprocally occupy definite relationships of production. They are independent and equal producers of private "labors." But these private "labors" are of a peculiar kind, inasmuch as they are effected, not for personal use but for exchange, inasmuch as they are intended for the satisfaction, not of individual need, but of social need. Thus whereas private ownership and the division of labor reduces society into its atoms, the exchange of products restores to society its social interconnections.

The term commodity, therefore, is an *economic* term; it is the expression of social relationships between mutually independent producers in so far as these relationships are effected through the instrumentality of goods. The contrasted qualities of the commodity as use value and as value, the contrast between its manifestation as a natural form or as a value form, now appears to us to be a contrast between the commodity manifesting itself on the one hand as a *natural* thing and on the other hand as a *social* thing. We have, in fact, to do with a dichotomy, wherein the giving of the place of honor to one branch excludes the other, and conversely. But the difference is merely one of point of view. The commodity is a unity of use value and of value, but we can regard that unity from two different aspects. As a natural thing, it is the object of a natural science; as a social thing, it is the object of a social science, the object of political economy. The object of political economy is the social aspect of the commodity, of the good, in

15

so far as it is a symbol of social interconnection. On the other hand, the natural aspect of the commodity, its use value, lies outside the domain of political economy. [4]

A commodity, however, can be the expression of social relationships only in so far as it is itself contemplated as a product of society, as a thing on which society has stamped its imprint. But for society, which exchanges nothing, the commodity is nothing more than a product of labor. Moreover, the members of society can only enter into economic relationships one with another according as they work one for another. This material relationship appears in its historic form as the exchange of commodities. The total product of labor presents itself as a total value, which in individual commodities manifests itself quantitatively as exchange value.

The commodity being, as far as society is concerned, the product of labor, this labor thereby secures its specific character as socially necessary labor; the commodity no longer exhibits itself to us as the product of the labor of different subjects, for these must now rather be looked upon as simple "instruments of labor." Economically regarded, therefore, the private "labors" manifest themselves as their opposites, as social "labors." The condition which gives its value-creating quality to labor is, therefore, the social determination of the labor—it is a quality of social labor.

Thus the process of abstraction whereby Marx passes from the concept of concrete private labor to the concept of abstractly human social labor, far from being, as Böhm-Bawerk imagines, identical with the process of abstraction whereby Marx excludes use value from consideration, is in fact the very opposite of that process.

A use value is an individual relationship between a thing and a human being. If I disregard its concreteness (and I am compelled to do so as soon as I alienate the thing so that it ceases to be a use value for me) I thereby destroy this individual relationship. But solely in its individuality can a use value be

16

the measure of my personal estimate of value. If, on the other hand, I disregard the concrete manner in which I have expended my labor, it nevertheless remains a fact that labor in general has been expended in its universal human form, and this is an objective magnitude the measure of which is furnished by the duration of the effort.

It is precisely this objective magnitude with which Marx is concerned. He is endeavoring to discover the social nexus between the apparently isolated agents of production. Social production, and therewith the actual material basis of society, is, according to its nature, qualitatively determined by the nature of the organization of social labor. This organization, causally determined by economic need, soon acquires a legal, a juristic fixation. An "external regulation" of this character constitutes a logical premise of the economic system, and furnishes the framework within which the separate elements of the society, the elements which labor and the elements which control labor, mutually influence one another. In a society characterized by the division of property and by the division of labor, this relationship appears in the form of exchange, expresses itself as exchange value. The social nexus manifests itself as the outcome of private relationships, the relationships not of private individuals but of private things. It is precisely this which involves the whole problem in mystery. Inasmuch, however, as the things enter into mutual relations, the private labor which has produced them acquires validity solely in so far as it is an expenditure of its own antithesis, socially necessary labor.

The outcome of the social process of production thus qualitatively determined is quantitatively determined by the sum total of the expended social labor. As an aliquot part of the social product of labor (and as such only does the commodity function in exchange), the individual commodity is quantitatively determined by the quota of social labor time embodied in it.

As a value, therefore, the commodity is socially

determined, is a social thing. As such alone can it be subjected to economic consideration. But when our task is to effect the economic analysis of any social institution that we may discover the intimate law of motion of the society, and when we call upon the law of value to render us this service, the principle of value cannot be any other than that to whose variations the changes in the social institution must in the last instance be referred.

Every theory of value which starts from use value, that is to say from the natural qualities of the thing, whether from its finished form as a useful thing or from its function, the satisfaction of a want, starts from the individual relationship between a thing and a human being instead of starting from the social relationships of human beings one with another. This involves the error of attempting from the subjective individual relationship, therefrom subjective estimates of value are properly deducible, to deduce an objective social measure. Inasmuch as this individual relationship is equally present in all social conditions, inasmuch as it does not contain within itself any principle of change (for the development of the wants and the possibility of their satisfaction are themselves likewise determined), we must, if we adopt such a procedure, renounce the hope of discovering the laws of motion and the evolutionary tendencies of society. Such an outlook is unhistorical and unsocial. Its categories are natural and eternal categories.

Marx, conversely, starts from labor in its significance as the constitutive element in human society, as the element whose development determines in the final analysis the development of society. In his principle of value he thus grasps the factor by whose quality and quantity, by whose organization and productive energy, social life is causally controlled. The fundamental economic idea is consequently identical with the fundamental idea of the materialist conception of history. Necessarily so, seeing that economic life is but a part of historic life, so that conformity to law in economics must be the same as conformity to law in history. To the extent that labor in its social form becomes the measure of value, economics is established as a social and historical science. Therewith the purview of economic science is restricted to the definite epoch of social evolution wherein the good becomes a commodity. In other words, it is restricted to the epoch wherein labor and the power which controls labor have not been consciously elevated to the rank of a regulative principle of social metabolism and social predominance, but wherein this principle unconsciously and automatically establishes itself as a material quality of things—inasmuch as, as the outcome of the peculiar form which social metabolism has assumed in exchange, it results that private labors acquire validity only in so far as they are social labors. *Society has, as it were, assigned to each of its members the quota of labor necessary to society; has specified to each individual how much labor he must expend.* And these individuals have forgotten what their quota was, and rediscover it only in the process of social life.

It is therefore because labor is the social bond uniting an atomized society, and not because labor is the matter most technically relevant, that labor is the principle of value and that the law of value is endowed with reality. It is precisely because Marx takes socially necessary labor as his starting point that he is so well able to discover the inner working of a society based on private property and the division of labor. For him the individual relation between human being and good is a premise. What he sees in exchange is not a difference of individual estimates, but the equation of a historically determined relationship of production. Only in this relationship of production, as the symbol, as the material expression, of personal relationships, as the bearer of social labor, does the good become a commodity; and only *as the expression of derivative relationships of production* can things which are not the products of labor assume the character of commodities.

We thus reach Böhm-Bawerk's objection as expressed in his inquiry, How can the products of nature have "exchange value"? The natural conditions under which labor is performed are unalterably given to society, and from these conditions therefore changes in social relationships cannot be derived. The only thing that changes is the manner in which labor is applied to these natural conditions. The degree to which such application is successful determines the productivity of labor. The change in productivity is effected solely by the concrete labor which creates use value; but according as the mass of products wherein the value-creating labor is embodied increases or diminishes, it results that more or less labor than before is embodied in the individual specimen. To the extent that natural energy is at an individual's disposal, so that he is thereby enabled to labor with a productivity exceeding the social average, that individual is in a position to realize an extra surplus value. This extra surplus value, capitalized, then manifests itself as the price of this natural energy (it may be of the soil) whose appurtenance it is. The soil is not a commodity, but in a lengthy historical process it acquires the characteristics of a commodity as a condition requisite to the production of commodities. The expressions "value of land" or "price of land" are therefore nothing more than irrational formulas beneath which is concealed a real relationship of production, that is to say a relationship of value. The ownership of land does not create the portion of value which is transformed into surplus profit; it merely enables the landowner to transfer this surplus profit from the manufacturer's pocket to his own. But Böhm-Bawerk, who ascribes to the gifts of nature a value peculiar to themselves, is a prey to the physiocrats' illusion that rent is derived from nature and not from society.

Thus Böhm-Bawerk continually confuses the natural and the social. This is plainly shown in his enunciation of the additional qualities common to commodities. It is a strange medley: the fact of appropriation is the legal expression of the historical relationships which must be presupposed in order that goods may be exchanged at all (it is "pre-economic" fact)—though how this should be a quantitative measure remains inexplicable. It is a natural quality of commodities to be natural

20

products, but in no way does this render them quantitatively comparable. Inasmuch, further, as they are the objects of demand and have a relationship to demand, they acquire a use value; for relative scarcity renders them subjectively the objects of esteem, whereas objectively (from the standpoint of society) their scarcity is a function of the cost of labor, securing therein its objective measure in the magnitude or its cost.

Just as in the foregoing Böhm-Bawerk fails to distinguish the natural qualities of commodities from their social qualities, so in the further course of his criticism he confuses the outlook on labor in so far as it creates use value with the outlook on labor in so far as it creates value; and he proceeds to discover a new contradiction in the law of value–though Marx "with a masterly dialectic ... seeks to suggest" that the facts "do not contain a contradiction of his fundamental principle, but are only a slightly different reading of it."

Marx declares that skilled labor is equivalent to a definite quantity of unskilled labor. He has however taught us, says Böhm-Bawerk, that things equated with one another by exchange "contain equal amounts of some common factor, and this common factor must be labor and working time." But the facts before us, he says, do not comply at all with this demand. For in skilled labor, for example in the product of a sculptor, there is no unskilled labor at all, and still less can we say that the unskilled labor equal to the five days' labor of the stonebreaker is embodied in the sculptor's product. "The plain truth is [very plain indeed!–R. H.] that the two products embody different Kinds of labor in different amounts, and every unprejudiced person will admit that this means a state of things exactly contrary to the conditions which Marx demands and must affirm, namely, that they embody labor of the *same kind* and of the *same amount.*"

Let me parenthetically remark that there is no question here of the "same amount," no question of *quantitative equality.* We are solely concerned with the comparability of different

21

kinds of labor, that is to say with the possibility of expressing them in terms of some common measure, with the possibility of their *qualitative* equalization.

It is true, continues Böhm-Bawerk, that Marx says: "Experience shows that this reduction [from skilled to unskilled labor] is constantly being made. A commodity may be the product of the most skilled labor, but its value, by equating it to the product of simple unskilled labor, represents a definite quantity of the latter labor alone. The different proportions in which different sorts of labor are reduced to unskilled labor as their standard are established by a social process that goes on behind the backs of the producers, and, consequently, appear to be fixed by custom." [5]

Böhm-Bawerk, however, inquires, what is the meaning of the appeal to "value" and the "social process" as the determining factors of the standard of reduction? "Apart from everything else, it simply means that Marx is arguing in a circle. The real subject of inquiry is the exchange relations of commodities," why, for instance, the sculptor's work is worth five times as much as the unskilled labor of the stone-breaker. "Marx... says that the exchange relation is this, and no other– because one day of sculptor's work is reducible exactly to five days' unskilled work. And why is it reducible to exactly five days? Because experience shows that it is so reduced by a social process." But it is this very process which requires explanation. Were the exchange relationship 1:3 instead of 1:5, "Marx would equally bid us accept the rate of reduction of 1:3 as the one derived from experience; ... in short, it is clear that we shall never learn in this way the actual reasons why products of different kinds of work should be exchanged in this or that proportion." In this decisive point, says the critic, the law of value breaks down.

We have here a statement of the familiar difficulty, the difficulty to which others besides Böhm-Bawerk have drawn attention. In the preface to the first volume of *Capital,* Marx, with his well-known "social optimism," presupposes "a reader who is willing to learn something new, and therefore to think for himself"– this being I believe the only unwarranted presupposition Marx ever made. But every thoughtful reader will at the outset feel that there is a gap in the argument, and the void has been indicated by "more or less Marxist" writers, as by Bernstein, C. Schmidt, and Kautsky.

Let us regard the matter more closely. First of all, Böhm-Bawerk himself tells us that the difference consists only in this, that in the one case we have to do with skilled and in the other with unskilled labor. It is obvious, therefore, that the difference in value of the respective products must depend upon a difference in the labor. The same natural product is in one case the object upon which skilled labor has been expended, and in the other case the object upon which unskilled labor has been expended, and it acquires a different value in the respective cases. Thus there is no *logical* objection to the law of value. The only question that arises is whether it is necessary to determine the ratio of value between the two kinds of labor, and whether the difficulty of effecting this determination may not prove insuperable. For, if we assume a knowledge of the ratio to be indispensable, in the absence of such knowledge the concept of value will be incapable of furnishing the explanation of economic processes.

Let us reconsider Marx's argument. In the passage previously quoted we read: "Its value [that is to say the value of the product of skilled labor], by equating it to the product of simple unskilled labor, represents a definite quantity of the latter labor alone." For this process to be comprehensible, however, value theory must regard the labor available for society at any given moment as composed of homogeneous parts–individual labor, in so far as it creates value, being merely an aliquot part of this quantitative whole. But only if I am able to express this whole in terms of some common unit of measurement can I regard it as qualitatively homogeneous. The required unit of measurement is furnished by "simple average labor," and this "is the expenditure of simple labor power, that is, of the labor power which on the average, apart from any special development, exists in the organism of every ordinary individual." [6] Skilled labor counts as a multiple of this unit of simple average labor. But what multiple? This, says Marx, is established by a social process that goes on behind the backs of the producers. Now Böhm-Bawerk will not admit that this appeal to experience is valid, and declares that here the theory of value breaks down utterly. For "in what proportions skilled is to be translated into terms of unskilled labor in the valuation of their respective products is not determined, nor can it be determined, a priori, by any property inherent in the skilled labor itself, but it is the actual result alone which decides the actual exchange relations." [7] Thus Böhm-Bawerk demands that the ratio should enable him to determine in advance the absolute height of prices, for in his view, as he elsewhere tells us, the essential task of economics is to explain the phenomenon of price.

Is it really true, however, that in default of a knowledge of the ratio, the law of value becomes unworkable? In striking contrast with Böhm-Bawerk, Marx looks upon the theory of value, not as the means for ascertaining prices, but as the means for discovering the laws of motion of capitalist society. Experience teaches us that the *absolute* height of prices is the starting point of this movement, but, for the rest, the absolute height of prices remains a matter of secondary importance, and we are concerned merely with studying the law of their variation. It is a matter of indifference whether any specific kind of skilled labor is to be reckoned the fourfold multiple or the sixfold multiple of unskilled labor. The important point is that a doubling or trebling of productive power in the sphere of skilled labor would lower the product of skilled labor twofold or threefold vis-a-vis the product of unskilled labor (by hypothesis unchanged).

The *absolute* height of prices is given us by experience; what interests us is the *law-abiding variation* that these prices

24

undergo. Like all variations, this variation is brought about by a force; and since we have to do with changes in social phenomena, these changes must be effected by variations in the magnitude of a social force, the social power of production.

Since, however, the law of value discloses to us that in the final analysis this development of productive power controls variations in prices, it becomes possible for us to grasp the laws of these changes; and since all economic phenomena manifest themselves by changes in prices, it is further possible to attain to an understanding of economic phenomena in general. Ricardo, aware of the incompleteness of his analysis of the law of value, therefore declares in so many words that the investigation to which he wishes to direct the reader's attention concerns variations in the relative value of commodities and not variations in their absolute value.

It follows that the lack of a knowledge of the ratio in question by no means restricts the importance of the law of value as a means by which we are enabled to recognize the conformity to law displayed by the economic mechanism. In another respect, however, this lack would be serious. If in practice the absolute height of price had in the first instance to be established by the social process, the concept of value would have to contain all the elements which *theoretically* allow us to apprehend the process whereby society effectuates the reduction of skilled labor to unskilled. Otherwise this process, which exercises a decisive influence upon the magnitude of value, though it would indeed positively exist and would not involve any contradiction to the law of value, would nevertheless afford an explanation of a part only (and that the most important) of economic phenomena, but would leave unexplained another part, namely the starting point of these variations.

When, however, Böhm-Bawerk inquires, what is the quality *inherent* in skilled labor which gives that labor its peculiar power to create value, the question is wrongly stated. The value-creating quality is not per se inherent in any labor.

25

Solely in conjunction with a definite mode of social organization of the process of production does labor create value. Hence, we cannot attain to the concept of value-creating labor merely by contemplating isolated labor in its concreteness. Skilled labor, therefore, if I am to regard it as value-creating, must not be contemplated in isolation, but as part of social labor.

The question consequently arises, what is skilled labor from the social standpoint? Only when we can answer this can we expect to attain to a position from which we shall be able to recognize the principles according to which the aforesaid social reduction can be effected. Manifestly these principles can be none other than those which are contained in the law of value. But here we encounter a difficulty. The law of value applies to commodities, whereas labor is not a commodity even though it appears as such when we speak of the wage of labor. Only labor *power* is a commodity and possesses value; labor *creates* value but does not itself possess value. It is not difficult to calculate the value of a labor *power* engaged on skilled work; like every other commodity it is equal to the labor requisite for its production and reproduction, and this is composed of the cost of maintenance and the cost of training. But here we are not concerned with the value of a skilled labor power, but with the question how and in what ratio skilled labor creates more value than unskilled.

We must not deduce the higher value which skilled labor creates from the higher wage of skilled labor power, for this would be to deduce the value of the product from the "value of labor." It is true that Bernstein [8] proposes to do this, and believes that he can justify himself by a quotation from Marx. But if we read the sentence in the context from which Bernstein has torn it, we see that it conveys the precise opposite of that which Bernstein wishes to deduce from it. Marx writes: "It has previously been pointed out that, as far as the process of producing surplus value is concerned, it is a matter of absolutely no moment whether the labor appropriated by the capitalist be average unskilled social labor or comparatively skilled labor, labor of a higher specific gravity. The labor which, when contrasted with average social labor, counts as higher, comparatively skilled labor, is the manifestation of a labor power to the making of which higher formative costs have gone, whose production has cost more labor time, and which consequently has a higher value than that possessed by unskilled labor power. Now whereas the value of this power is higher, it must also be remembered that it manifests itself in higher work, and consequently materializes, in equal spaces of time, in comparatively higher values. Whatever difference in skill there may be between the labor of a spinner and that of a jeweler, the portion of his labor by which the jeweler merely replaces the value of his own labor power does not in any way differ in quality from the additional portion by which he creates surplus value. In the making of jewelry, just as in spinning, the surplus value results only from a quantitative excess of labor, from a lengthening out of one and the~ same labor process, in the one case of the process of making jewels, in the other of the process of making yarn." We see that the question Marx here discusses is how skilled labor can create surplus value despite the high wage, despite, that is to say, the magnitude of the necessary labor. Expressed in fuller detail, the thoughts in the sentence quoted by Bernstein would read somewhat as follows: "Even though the value of this power be higher, it can none the less produce more surplus value, because it manifests itself in higher work"–and so on.

Marx leaves out the intermediate clause and introduces what follows with the word *"aber"* ["but"],whereas, if Bernstein had been right, he would have had to use the word *"daher"* ["consequently," or "therefore"]. To deduce the value of the product of labor from the wage of labor conflicts grossly with the Marxist theory. The value of labor power being given, I should only be in a position to deduce the value which this labor power newly creates if I knew what had been the rate of exploitation. But even if the rate of exploitation of unskilled labor were known to me, I should have no right to assume that the identical rate of exploitation prevailed for skilled labor. For the latter, the rate of exploitation might be much lower. Thus neither directly nor indirectly does the wage of a skilled labor power give me any information regarding the value which this labor power newly creates. The visage which the Marxist theory would assume if Bernstein's interpretation were to be accepted (and Bernstein himself tells us that in his view the theory would assume an utterly different visage) would possess ironical lineaments which could hardly be concealed. We must, therefore, endeavor to approach the solution of the problem in a different manner. [9]

Average unskilled labor is the expenditure of unskilled labor power, but qualified or skilled labor is the expenditure of qualified labor power. For the production of this skilled labor power, however, a number of unskilled labors were requisite. These are stored up in the person of the qualified laborer, and not until he begins to work are these formative labors made fluid *on behalf of society*. The labor of the technical educator thus transmits, not only *value* (which manifests itself in the form of the higher wage), but in addition its own *value-creating power*. The formative labors are therefore *latent as far as society is concerned*, and do not manifest themselves until the skilled labor power begins to work. Its expenditure consequently signifies the expenditure of all the different unskilled labors which are simultaneously condensed therein.

Unskilled labor, if applied to the production of a qualified or skilled labor power, creates on the one hand the value of this labor power, which reappears in the wage of the qualified' labor power; but on the other hand by the concrete method of its application it creates a new use value, which consists in this, that there is now available a labor power which can create value with all those potentialities possessed by the unskilled labors utilized in its formation. Inasmuch as unskilled labor is used in the formation of skilled labor, it thus creates on the one hand new value and transmits on the other to its product its use value–to be the source of new value. Regarded from the standpoint of society, unskilled labor is latent as long as it is utilized for the formation of skilled labor power. Its working for society does not begin until the skilled labor power it has helped to produce becomes active. Thus in this single act of the expenditure of skilled labor a sum of unskilled labors is expended, and in this way there is created a sum of value and surplus value corresponding to the total value which would have been created by the expenditure of all the unskilled labors which were requisite to produce the skilled labor power and its function, the skilled labor. From the standpoint of society, therefore, and economically regarded, skilled labor appears as a multiple of unskilled labor, however diverse skilled and unskilled labor may appear from some other outlook, physiological, technical, or aesthetic.

In what it has to give for the product of skilled labor, society consequently pays an equivalent for the value which the unskilled labors would have created had they been directly consumed by society.

The more unskilled labor that skilled labor embodies, the more does the latter create higher value, for in effect we have numerous unskilled labors simultaneously employed upon the formation of the same product. In reality, therefore, skilled labor is unskilled labor multiplied. An example may make the matter clearer. A man owns ten storage batteries wherewith he can drive ten different machines. For the manufacture of a new product he requires another machine for which a far greater motive power is requisite. He now employs the ten batteries to charge a single accumulator, which is capable of driving the new machine. The powers of the individual batteries thereupon manifest themselves as a unified force in the new battery, a unified force which is the tenfold multiple of the simple average force.

A skilled labor may contain, not unskilled labors alone, but in addition skilled labors of a different kind, and these in their turn are reducible to unskilled labor. The greater the extent to which other skilled labors are incorporated in a skilled labor, the briefer will be its formative process.

Thus the Marxist theory of value enables us to recognize the principles in accordance with which the social process of reducing skilled labor to unskilled labor is effected. It therefore renders the magnitude of value *theoretically measurable*. But when Böhm-Bawerk insists that Marx ought to have furnished the empirical proof of his theory, and when he contends that the requisite proof would have consisted in demonstrating the relationship between exchange values or prices and quantities of labor, he is confusing theoretical with *practical* measurability. What I am able to determine by experience is the concrete expenditure of labor requisite for the production of a specified good. How far this concrete labor is socially necessary labor, how far, that is to say, it has a bearing on the formation of value, I am only able to determine if I know the actual average degree of productivity and intensity which the productive power has required, and if I also know what quantum of this good is demanded by society. This means that we are asking from the individual that which society performs. For society is the only accountant competent to calculate the height of prices, and the method which society employs to this end is the method of competition. Inasmuch as, in free competition on the market, society treats as a unity the concrete labor expended by all producers for the production of a good, and inasmuch as society only pays for labor in so far as its expenditure was socially necessary, it is society which first shows to what degree this concrete labor has actually collaborated in the formation of value and fixes the price accordingly. The utopia of "labor notes" and "constituted value" was based upon this very illusion that the theoretical standard of measurement is at the same time an immediately practical standard of measurement. This is the conception in accordance with which the theory of value is regarded, not as a means "for detecting the law of motion of contemporary society," but as a means of securing a price list that shall be as stable and as just as possible.

The search for such a price list led von Buch [10] to a theory which, in order to determine price, needs nothing more than this–a knowledge of the price. But the psychological theory of "value" is in no better case.

That theory indicates the various degrees of satisfaction of needs with definite but arbitrarily selected figures, and arranges that these figures shall signify the prices which people are willing to pay for the means wherewith needs are satisfied. This more effectually conceals the process whereby a number of arbitrary prices are assumed instead of a single arbitrary price.

The empirical proof of the accuracy of the theory of value lies in a very different direction from that towards which Böhm-Bawerk directs his inquiries. If the theory of value is to be the key for the understanding of the capitalist mode of production, it must be able to explain the phenomena of that mode of production in a manner free from contradictions. The actual processes of the capitalist world must not conflict with the theory but must confirm it. According to Böhm-Bawerk the theory fails in this respect. The third volume of *Capital,* in which Marx has no longer been able to ignore the actual processes, shows that these actual processes could not be harmonized with the presuppositions of the theory of value. The data of the third volume are in crass contradiction with those of the first volume. The theory is shipwrecked on the rocks of reality. For reality, says Böhm-Bawerk, shows that the law of value has no validity for the process of exchange, seeing that commodities are exchanged at prices which permanently diverge from the value of the commodities. In the discussion of the problem of the average rate of profit the contradiction becomes obvious. Marx can solve this problem only by the simple abandonment of his theory of value. This reproach of self-contradiction has become a commonplace of bourgeois economics since it was made by Böhm-Bawerk. When we are criticizing Böhm-Bawerk we are criticizing the representatives of bourgeois criticism of the third volume of *Capital.*

Footnotes

1. *Geschichte und Kritik der Kapitalzins-Theorien,* 2nd ed., pp. 511 ff. Above, pp. 68 ff.

2. Vol. I, p. 100.

3. Vol. I, p. 45.

4. "That is the reason why German compilers are so fond of dwelling on use value, calling it a 'good.'... For intelligent information on 'goods' one must turn to treatises on commodities." Marx, *A Contribution to the Critique of Political Economy,* Kerr ed., p. 21n.

5. Vol. I, pp. 51-52.

6. Vol. I, p. 51.

7. Above, p. 83.

8. Eduard Bernstein, "Zur Theorie des Arbeitswerts," *Die Neue Zeit,* Vol. XVIII (1899-1900), Part I, p. 359.

9. The translators had hoped to avoid burdening Hilferding's text with any extended notes of their own, but they find it necessary to draw attention to a strange discrepancy between the text of the fourth (German) edition of *Capital,* finally revised by Engels in 1890, and the third edition, that of 1883, the one quoted above by Hilferding. In the third edition, the sentence about which the trouble arises runs as follows (p. 178): *"Ist der Wert dieser Kraft höher, so aussert sie sich aber auch in höherer Arbeit und vergegenstandlicht sich daher, in denselben Zeitraumen, in verhaltnissmassig höheren Wert."* Our translation of this, which we prefer to that found on page 179 of Moore & Aveling's version, runs as follows: "Now whereas the value of this power is higher, it must also be remembered that it manifests itself in higher work, and consequently materializes, in equal spaces of time, in comparatively higher values." The phrase "it must be remembered that" seems rather a lengthy rendering of the German "aber," but in this particular context that phrase effectively presents the precise shade of meaning.

Next let us turn to Bernstein. This writer quotes from the second (German) edition of *Capital,* in which (p. 186) the passage cited is identical with that quoted from the third edition by Hilferding. But Bernstein interpolates an exclamation mark expressive almost of derision, the passage thus reading: "Now whereas the value of this power is higher, it must also be remembered that it manifests itself in higher work, and consequently [!] materializes in equal spaces of time, in comparatively higher values." Thereafter (writing in *Die Neue Zeit* of December 23, 1899) Bernstein continues: "Here the value of the labor power which materializes in the wage of labor appears to be decisive for the value of the product. Were we to accept this as universally valid, the Marxist theory of value would in my opinion assume a visage utterly different from that which, as presented by all its expositors, it has hitherto assumed. It would differ from the theory as expounded by Marx himself, for Marx, in his essay *Value, Price, and Profit* expressly declares: 'To determine the values of commodities by the relative quantities of labor fixed in them, is, therefore, a thing quite different from the tautological method of determining the values of commodities by the value of labor, or by wages' [International Publishers' ed., p. 32]. However this may be, here is a point which still remains to be cleared up, unless it be imagined that the elucidation is to be found in the disquisitions of the third volume concerning cost price and price of production which, just like the fact of surplus value, do not require for their establishment the labor theory of value in its original form."

What Hilferding has to say of Bernstein we have seen in the text. The reader will note more particularly Hilferding's contention that were Bernstein right, Marx would have written "daher" in place of "aber." Now comes the point justifying the introduction of the present note. In the fourth (German) edition of *Capital* (p. 160) the word "aber" has been changed to "daher," not in consequence of what Bernstein wrote in *Die Neue Zeit* in 1899, for Engels' preface to the fourth edition is dated June 25, 1890. Further, in this preface, Engels gives a detailed specification of the important alterations in the text of the fourth edition, making no direct allusion to the change on page 160, but adding: "Other trifling modifications are of a purely technical nature." We take it this means trifling improvements in literary style. In any case it would seem clear that Engels did not regard this particular alteration as important. The revised sentence may best be rendered as follows: "Now if the value of this power be higher, the result is that it manifests itself in higher work, and consequently it materializes in equal spaces of time, in comparatively higher values."

Marx and Engels are beyond our reach. For the moment we are unable to communicate with Bernstein in Berlin or with Hilferding in Vienna. We must leave the problems raised anent this disputed text to the ingenuity of the English-speaking Marxists. They must sharpen their weapons, and make ready to deal with both the German and the Austrian commentators when the foolish capitalist bickering which at present hampers communications shall at length have drawn to a dose. Among other things, they will want to know why Hilferding, writing in 1903, did not consult the definitive fourth edition of Capital, published thirteen years earlier!–E. & C.

P.

10. *Die Intensitat der Arbeit,* Leipzig, 1896.

Chapter II
Value and Average Profit

THE problem with which we are now concerned is familiar. In the various spheres of production the organic composition of capital, the ratio between *c* (constant capital, expended on the means of production) and *v* (variable capital, expended in paying the wage of labor), varies. Since, however, only variable capital produces new value, and since, therefore, it alone produces surplus value, the amount of surplus value produced by two capitals of equal size varies in accordance with the organic composition of these respective capitals, varies, that is to say, in accordance with variations in the ratio between the constant capital and the variable capital in the respective enterprises. But, therewith, also, the rate of profit, the ratio between the surplus value and the total capital, varies. Thus according to the law of value equal capitals yield different profits proportionate to the magnitudes of the living labor which they set in motion. This conflicts with reality, for in the real world equal capitals bring identical profits, whatever their composition. How can the "contradiction" be explained?

Let us first hear what Marx has to say.

"The whole difficulty arises from the fact that commodities are not exchanged simply as *commodities,* but as *products of capital* which claim equal shares of the total amount of surplus value, if they are of equal magnitude, or shares proportional to their different magnitudes." [1]

The capital advanced for the production of a commodity constitutes the cost price of this commodity. "The cost price [= c + V] does not show the distinction between variable and constant capital to the capitalist. A commodity, for which he must advance £100 in production, costs him the same amount whether he invests 90c + 10v, or 10c + 90v. He always spends

£100 for it, no more no less. The cost prices are the same for investment of the same amounts of capital in different spheres, no matter how much the produced values and surplus values may differ. The equality of cost prices is the basis for the competition of the invested capitals, by which an average rate of profit is brought about." [2]

To elucidate the working of capitalist competition Marx presents the following table, wherein the rates of surplus value s/v are assumed to be identical, while as regards the constant capital varying proportions are incorporated into the product according as the wear and tear varies.

Capitals	Rate of Surplus Value, Percent	Surplus Value	Rate of Profit, Percent	Used-up C	Value of Commodities
I 80c + 20c	100	20	20	50	90
II 70c + 30v	100	30	30	51	111
III 60c + 40v	100	40	40	51	131
IV 85c + 15v	100	15	15	40	70
V 95c + 5v	100	5	5	10	20

In this table we see five instances in which the total capital is identical, and in which the degree of exploitation of labor is the same in every case, but the rates of profit vary widely, according to the differing organic composition. Let us now look upon these capitals, invested in various fields, as a single capital, of which numbers I to V merely constitute component parts (more or less analogous to the different departments of a cotton mill which has different proportions of constant and of variable capital in its carding, preparatory spinning, spinning, and weaving rooms, on the basis of which the average proportion for the whole factory is calculated), then we should have a total capital of 500, a surplus value of 110, and a total value of commodities of 610. The average composition of the capital would be 500, made up of 390c and 110v, or in percentages, 78c and 22v. If each of the capitals of

36

100 were to be regarded simply as one fifth of the total capital, the average composition of each portion would be 78c and 22v, and in like manner to each 100 of capital would be allotted a mean surplus value of 22, so that the mean rate of profit would be 22 percent. The commodities must, then, be sold as follows:

Capitals	Surplus Value	Used-up C	Value of Commodities	Cost Price of Commodities	Price of Commodities	Rate of Profit, Percent	Deviation of Price from Value
I 80c + 20c	20	50	90	70	92	22	+ 2
II 70c + 30v	30	51	111	81	103	22	- 8
III 60c + 40v	40	51	131	91	113	22	- 18
IV 85c + 15v	15	40	70	55	77	22	+ 7
V 95c + 5v	5	10	20	15	37	22	+ 17

The commodities are thus sold at 2 + 7 + 17 = 26 above, and 8 + 18 = 26 below, their value, so that the deviations of prices from values mutually balance one another by the uniform distribution of the surplus value, or by the addition of the average profit of 22 percent of advanced capital to the respective cost prices of the commodities of I to V. One portion of the commodities is sold in the same proportion above in which the other is sold below value. Only the sale of the commodities at such prices renders it possible that the rate of profit for all five capitals shall uniformly be 22 percent, without regard to the organic composition of these capitals.

"Since the capitals invested in the various lines of production are of a different organic composition, and since the different percentages of the variable portions of these total capitals set in motion very different quantities of labor, it follows that these capitals appropriate very different quantities of surplus labor, or produce very different quantities of surplus

37

value. Consequently the rates of profit prevailing in the various lines of production are originally very different. These different rates of profit are equalized by means of competition into a general rate of profit, which is the average of all these special rates of profit. The profit allotted according to this average rate of profit to any capital, whatever may be its organic composition, is called the average profit. That price of any commodity which is equal to its cost price plus that share of average profit on the total capital invested (not merely consumed) in its production which is allotted to it in proportion to its conditions of turnover, is called its price of production. ... While the capitalists in the various spheres of production recover the value of the capital consumed in the production of their commodities through the sale of these, they do not secure the surplus value, and consequently the profit, created in their own sphere by the production of these commodities, but only as much surplus value, and profit, as falls to the share of every aliquot part of the total social capital out of the total social surplus value, or social profit produced by the total capital of society in all spheres of production. Every 100 of any invested capital, whatever may be its organic composition, draws as much profit during one year, or any other period of time, as falls to the share of every 100 of the total social capital during the same period. The various capitalists, so far as profits are concerned, are so many stockholders in a stock company in which the shares of profit are uniformly divided for every 100 shares of capital, so that profits differ in the case of the individual capitalists only according to the amount of capital invested by each one of them in the social enterprise, according to his investment in social production as a whole, according to his shares" (III, 186-187). The average profit is nothing other than the profit on the average social capital; its total, like the total of the surplus values, and like the prices determined by the addition of this average profit to the cost prices, are nothing other than the values transformed into prices of production. In the simple production of commodities, values are the center of gravity round which prices fluctuate. But "under capitalist

38

production it is not a question of merely throwing a certain mass of values into circulation and exchanging that mass for equal values in some other form, whether of money or other commodities, but it is also a question of advancing capital in production and realizing on it as much surplus value, or profit, in proportion to its magnitude, as any other capital of the same or of other magnitudes in whatever line of production. It is a question, then, of selling the commodities at least at prices which will yield the average profit, in other words, at prices of production. Capital comes in this form to a realization of *the social nature of its power,* in which every capitalist participates in proportion to his share in the total social capital....If the commodities are sold at their values...considerably different rates of profit arise in the various spheres of production...But capital withdraws from spheres with low rates of profit and invades others which yield a higher rate. By means of this incessant emigration and immigration, in a word by its distribution among the various spheres in response to a rise in the rate of profit here and its fall there, it brings about such a proportion of supply to demand that the average profit in the various spheres of production becomes the same, so that values are converted into prices of production" (III, 229-230).

In what relationship does this doctrine of the third volume stand to the celebrated law of value of the first volume?

In Böhm-Bawerk's opinion the third volume of *Capital* manifestly contains the statement of an actual and irreconcilable contradiction to the law of value, and furnishes proof that the equal average rate of profit can only become established if and because the alleged law of value does not hold good. In the first volume, declares Böhm-Bawerk, [3] it was maintained with the greatest emphasis that all value is based on labor and labor alone; the value was declared to be the common factor which appears in the exchange relation of commodities. We were told, in the form and with the emphasis of a stringent syllogistic conclusion, allowing of no exception, that to set down two commodities as equivalents in exchange implies that a common factor of the same magnitude exists in both, to which each of the two must be reducible. Apart, therefore, from temporary and occasional deviations, which are merely apparent breaches of the law of exchange of commodities, commodities which embody the same amount of labor must on principle, in the long run, exchange for each other. And now, in the third volume, we are told that what according to the teaching of the first volume must be, is not and never can be; that individual commodities do and must exchange with each other in a proportion different from that of the labor incorporated in them, and this not accidentally and temporarily, but of necessity and permanently.

But this, says Böhm-Bawerk, is no explanation and reconciliation of a contradiction, it is the naked contradiction itself. The theory of the average rate of profit and of the prices of production cannot be reconciled with the theory of value. Marx must himself have foreseen that this reproach would be made, and to this prevision is evidently due an anticipatory self-defense which, if not in form, yet in point of fact, is found in the Marxist system. He tries by a number of observations to render plausible the view that in spite of exchange relations being directly governed by prices of production, which differ from the values, all is nevertheless moving within the framework of the law of value, and that this law, in the last resort at least, governs prices. On this subject, however, Marx does not make use of his customary method, a formal, circumscribed demonstration, but gives only a number of juxtaposed casual remarks, containing divers arguments which are summed up by Böhm-Bawerk under four heads.

Before we consider these "arguments" and the counter-arguments of Böhm-Bawerk, it is necessary to say a word or two concerning the "contradiction" or the "withdrawal" which Marx is supposed to have perpetrated in the third volume. As regards the alleged withdrawal, those who use this term have forgotten that the first volume was not published until the tenth chapter of the third volume, which forms the bone of contention, had already been composed. For the draft of the last two books of *Capital* was composed by Marx during the years 1863 to 1867, and from a note by Engels (III, 209n) we learn that the tenth chapter of the third volume, the one containing the solution of the riddle, was written in 1865. To speak of a withdrawal in this connection is tantamount to saying that Marx, in order to remain at a definite point, first moved a mile forward and then a mile backward. Such is, nevertheless, the view which the vulgar economists have formed of the essence of the dialectic method, because they never see the process but only the completed result, so that the method always seems to them a mystical "hocus-pocus." Nor is there any better justification for the accusation of contradiction than for the accusation of withdrawal.

In Böhm-Bawerk's view, the contradiction is found in this, that, according to the first volume, only commodities embodying equivalent amounts of labor are exchanged each for the other, whereas in the third volume we are told that the individual commodities are exchanged one for another in ratios which do not correspond to the ratios between the amounts of labor respectively incorporated in them. Who denies it? If Marx had really maintained that, apart from irregular oscillations, commodities could only be exchanged one for another because equivalent quantities of labor are incorporated in them, or only in the ratios corresponding to the amounts of labor incorporated in them, Böhm-Bawerk would be perfectly right. But in the first volume Marx is only discussing exchange relationships as they manifest themselves when commodities are exchanged for their *values;* and solely on this supposition do the commodities embody equivalent quantities of labor. But exchange for their values is not a condition of exchange in general, even though, under certain specific historical conditions, exchange for corresponding values is indispensable, if these historical conditions are to be perpetually reproduced by the mechanism of social life. Under changed historical conditions, modifications of exchange ensue, and the only question is whether these modifications are to be regarded as taking place

41

according to law, and whether they can be represented as modifications of the law of value. If this be so, the law of value, though in modified form, continues to control exchange and the course of prices. All that is necessary is that we should understand the course of prices to be a modification of the pre-existing course of prices, which was under direct control of the law of value.

Böhm-Bawerk's mistake is that he confuses value with price, being led into this confusion by his own theory. Only if value (disregarding chance deviations, which may be neglected because they are mutually compensatory) were identical with price, would a permanent deviation of the prices of individual commodities from their values be a contradiction to the law of value. In the first volume, Marx already refers to the divergence of values from prices. Thus, he asks: "How can we account for the origin of capital on the supposition that prices are regulated by the average price, that is, ultimately by the value of the commodities?" And he adds: "I say 'ultimately,' because average prices do not directly coincide with the values of commodities, as Adam Smith, Ricardo, and others believe" (I, 185n). Again: "We have assumed that prices = values. We shall, however, see in Volume III, that even in the case of average prices the assumption cannot be made in this very simple manner" (I, 244n).

We thus see that the Marxist law of value is not canceled by the data of the third volume, but is merely modified in a definite way. We shall make closer acquaintance with these modifications and grasp their significance better after we have further considered the course of Böhm-Bawerk's exposition.

The first "argument" adduced by Marx in favor of his view is summarized by Böhm-Bawerk as follows:[4] Even if the separate commodities are being sold either above or below their values, these reciprocal fluctuations cancel each other, and in the community itself–taking into account all the branches of production–the total of the prices of production of the

42

commodities produced still remains equal to the sum of their values.

The first thing that strikes us here (and the observation may be repeated with regard to all that follows) is that Böhm-Bawerk denotes as an "argument" that which for Marx was no more than a logical deduction from his premises. It is then, of course, easy to demonstrate that what Marx says does not amount to an argument.

Böhm-Bawerk tells us that it is admitted by Marx that *individual* commodities do not exchange for one another at their values. Stress is laid on the fact that these individual deviations compensate or cancel each other. How much of the law of value is left? asks Böhm-Bawerk. The object of the law of value is to elucidate the actual exchange relations of commodities. We wish to know, for instance, why a coat should be worth as much in exchange as twenty yards of linen. There can clearly be a question of an exchange relationship only between *individual commodities among each other.* As soon, however, as we look at *all commodities as a whole* and sum up their prices, we must studiously and perforce avoid looking at the relations existing within this whole. The relative differences of price compensate each other in the sum total. It is, therefore, no answer to our question concerning the exchange relationships of the commodities to be told the total price which they bring when taken together. The state of the case is this: to the question of the problem of value, the Marxists first reply with their law of value, telling us that commodities exchange in proportion to the labor time embodied in them. They then revoke this answer as far as it concerns the domain of the exchange of individual commodities, the one domain in which the problem has any meaning, while they maintain it in full force only for the aggregate national product, for a domain therefore in which the problem, being without object, cannot properly be put at all. As an answer to the strict question of the problem of value, the law of value is avowedly contradicted by the facts; and in the only application in which it is not contradicted by them, it is no longer an answer to the question which demanded a solution. It is no answer at all, it is mere tautology. When one penetrates the disguises due to the use of money, commodities do eventually exchange for commodities. The aggregate of commodities is thus identical with the aggregate of the prices paid for them; or the price of the entire national product is nothing else than the national product itself. In these circumstances, therefore, it is quite true that the total price paid for the entire national product coincides precisely with the total amount of value or labor crystallized therein. But this tautological utterance denotes no increase of true knowledge, neither does it prove the correctness of the law that commodities exchange in proportion to the labor embodied in them. Thus Böhm-Bawerk.

The entire train of reasoning is utterly beside the point. Marx is inquiring about the total value, and his critic complains because he is not inquiring about the value of the individual commodity. Böhm-Bawerk fails to see what Marx is aiming at in this demonstration. It is important to show that the sum total of the prices of production is identical with the sum total of the values, because thereby, first of all, it is shown that the total price of production cannot be greater than the total value; but, inasmuch as the process of the production of value is effected solely within the sphere of production, this signifies that all profit originates from production and not from circulation, not from any addition to the finished product subsequently effected by the capitalist. Secondly, we learn that, since the total price is equal to the total value, the total profit cannot be anything else than the total surplus value. The total profit is thereby quantitatively determined, and solely on the basis of this determination does it become possible to calculate the magnitude of the rate of profit.

But can we, without lapsing into absurdity, venture to speak of a total value at all? Böhm-Bawerk confounds the exchange value with the value. Value manifests itself as exchange value, as a quantitatively determined relationship, in virtue of the fact that one commodity can be exchanged for

44

another. But whether, for example, a coat can be exchanged for twenty yards of linen cloth or for forty yards is not a matter of chance, but depends upon objective conditions, upon the amount of socially necessary labor time contained in the coat and in the linen respectively. These conditions must make themselves felt in the process of exchange, they must substantially control that process, and they must have an independent existence quite apart from exchange, if we are to be entitled to speak of the total value of commodities. [5]

Böhm-Bawerk overlooks the fact that value in the Marxist sense is an objective, quantitatively determined magnitude. He overlooks it because in reality the concept of value as determined by the marginal utility theory lacks this quantitative definiteness. Even supposing that the value as equivalent to the marginal utility of each unit in an aggregate of goods is known to me, this value being determined by the utility of the last unit in this store of goods, this does not enable me to calculate the magnitude of the value of the total store. But if the value, in the Marxist sense, of a single unit be known to me, the value of the aggregate of these units is likewise known.

In the transition from the simple to the capitalist production of commodities, the distribution of the social product is what undergoes change. The distribution of the surplus value is now no longer effected in accordance with the measure of the labor power which the individual producer has in his particular sphere expended for the production of surplus value, but is regulated by the magnitude of the capital it has been necessary to advance in order to set in motion the labor that creates the surplus value. It is obvious that the change in the distribution makes no difference in the total amount of surplus value undergoing distribution, that the social relationship is unaltered, and that the change in the distribution comes to pass solely through a modification in the price of the individual commodities. It is further obvious that if we are to determine the amount of divergence, we must know, not only the magnitude of the surplus value, but also the magnitude and

45

indeed the *value* magnitude of the advanced capital. The law of value enables us to determine this magnitude. I can thus readily ascertain the deviations as soon as the value magnitudes are known to me. Value is consequently the necessary theoretical starting point whence we can elucidate the peculiar phenomenon of prices resulting from capitalist competition.

Böhm-Bawerk's entire polemic is therefore all the more fallacious inasmuch as Marx, when he inquires about the total value, does this solely in order to distinguish, within the total value, the individual parts which are important to the capitalist process of distribution. Marx's concern is with the value newly created within a period of production, and with the ratio in which this newly created value is distributed between the working class and the capitalist class, thus furnishing the revenues of the two great classes. It is therefore utterly false to say that Marx revokes the law of value as far as individual commodities are concerned, and maintains it in force solely for the aggregate of these commodities. Böhm-Bawerk is led to make this contention only because he fails to distinguish between value and price. The truth is, rather, that the law of value, directly valid for the social product and its parts, enforces itself only inasmuch as certain definite modifications, conformable to law, occur in the prices of the individual capitalistically-produced commodities–but these modifications can only be made comprehensible by the discovery of the social nexus, and the law of value renders us this service. Finally, it is pure gibberish for Böhm-Bawerk to say, as he does, that the aggregate of commodities is identical with the aggregate of the prices paid for them. Aggregate of commodities and aggregate of prices are incommensurable magnitudes. Marx says that the sum total of the values (not of the commodities) is equal to the sum total of the prices of production.In this case we have commensurability, inasmuch as prices and values are both expressions for different quantities of labor. For the total price of production can be compared with the total value only if, though quantitatively different, they are qualitatively homogeneous, both being the expression of materialized labor.

It is true that Böhm-Bawerk considers that in the ultimate analysis commodities exchange for commodities, and that this is why the aggregate of prices is identical with the aggregate of commodities. But here he disregards not only the price but also the value of the commodities. The question is, given an aggregate of commodities, by the piece, by weight, etc., how great is their value, or what is their price, since for the social product these are coincident. This value or price is the magnitude of a definite quantity of money,and is something completely different from the aggregate of commodities, Marx's inquiry relates to this magnitude, which must according to his theory incorporate an equal expenditure of labor with the aggregate of commodities.

The first "argument," like those that follow, is merely designed to indicate how far the law of value holds good directly, without modifications. Naturally, it is easy for Böhm-Bawerk to show that the modification of the law of value which Marx had previously indicated as a necessary outcome of the nature of capitalist competition, and which he here invariably presupposes, is not proved.

In his criticism of the second argument, Böhm-Bawerk proceeds as follows. Marx, he says, claims for the law of value that it governs the variation of prices, inasmuch as, if the labor time required for the production of commodities be reduced, prices fall; if it be increased, prices rise (III, 208, 211). But Böhm-Bawerk has omitted the condition which Marx attaches to this proposition, for Marx begins by saying: "Whatever may be the way in which the prices of the various commodities are first fixed or mutually regulated, the law of value always dominates their movements." Böhm-Bawerk overlooks this, and reproaches Marx with ignoring the fact that labor, while it is *one* of the determinants of price, is not the sole determinant, as Marx's theory demands. This conclusion, says Böhm-Bawerk, rests on an oversight so obvious that it is amazing Marx failed to perceive it. But what Marx said, and the only thing he wanted to say, was that changes in the expenditure of labor entail changes in prices, that is to say that, the prices being given, the variation in prices is determined by the variation in the productivity of labor. The oversight is here committed by Böhm-Bawerk, who could not have raised the objection he does had he quoted the passage in full.

More important, however, are Böhm-Bawerk's subsequent objections to the Marxist exposition. Marx conceives the transformation of value into price of production as an historical process, which is summarized by Böhm-Bawerk as the "third argument" in the following terms: "The law of value, Marx affirms, governs with undiminished authority the exchange of commodities in certain primary stages in which the change of values into prices of production has not yet been accomplished." The argument, we are told, has not been developed by Marx with precision and clearness, but the substance of it has been interwoven into his other disquisitions.

The conditions which are requisite in order that commodities shall be exchanged for their values are developed by Marx as follows: He assumes that the workers themselves own their respective means of production, that they labor on the average for an equal time with equal intensity, and that they exchange their commodities directly. Then two workmen in any one day will by their labor have added to their product equal amounts of new value, but the respective products will vary in value in accordance with variations in the amount of labor previously incorporated in the means of production. This latter portion of value will correspond to the constant capital of the capitalist economy; the portion of the new value expended upon the workers' means of subsistence will correspond to the variable capital; while the portion of the new value which remains will correspond to the surplus value, which will accrue to the laborer. Thus both the laborers receive equal values after the value of the invested "constant" capital has been deducted; but the relationship between the portion of value representing surplus value and the value of the means of production—that which corresponds to the capitalist rate of profit–will differ in the respective cases. Since, however, each of them has the value of the means of production made good to him in exchange, the circumstance is completely immaterial. "The exchange of commodities at their values, or approximately at their values, requires, therefore, a much lower stage than their exchange at their prices of production, which requires a relatively high development of capitalist production....Aside from the fact that prices and their movements are dominated by the law of value, it is quite appropriate, under these circumstances, to regard the value of commodities, not only theoretically, but also historically, as existing prior to the prices of production. This applies to conditions in which the laborer owns his means of production, and this is the condition of the land-owning farmer and of the craftsman in the old world as well as the modern world. This agrees also with the view formerly expressed by me that the development of product into commodities arises through the exchange between different communes, not through that between the members of the same commune. It applies not only to this primitive condition, but also to subsequent conditions based on slavery or serfdom, and to the guild organization of handicrafts, so long as the means of production installed in one line of production cannot be transferred to another line except under difficulties, so that the various lines of production maintain, to a certain degree, the same mutual relations as foreign countries or communistic groups" (III, 206-209).

Against this reasoning, Böhm-Bawerk tells us, "the gravest doubts arise, whether we regard it from within or without." It is inherently improbable, and experience also is against it. To demonstrate the improbability, Böhm-Bawerk illustrates Marx's example arithmetically. Laborer I, he says, represents a branch of production which requires technically a relatively large and costly preparatory means of production, for the installation of which he has required five years' labor, while the formation of the finished product needs an additional year.

Let us assume that the laborer furnishes the means of production. In that case it will be six years before he secures a return for the value of his labor. Laborer II, on the other hand, can provide the necessary means of production and complete the finished product in a single month, and will therefore secure his yield after one month. But in the Marxist hypothesis absolutely no attention is paid to this difference in point of time as regards the receipt of payment, whereas a year's postponement of the remuneration of labor is assuredly a circumstance demanding compensation. Unquestionably, says Böhm-Bawerk, the different branches of production are not equally accessible to all producers. Those branches which demand an extensive outlay of capital are accessible only to a dwindling minority. Hence, in these latter branches, there ensues a certain restriction in supply, and this ultimately forces the price of their products above the level of those branches which can be carried on without vexatious delays. Marx himself recognizes that in such cases exchange for values would lead to a disproportion. He records the admission by saying that the equivalent surplus values represent unequal rates of profit. But the question naturally arises, why this inequality should not be neutralized by competition just as it is in capitalist society. Marx answers the question by saying that the only thing which matters to the two laborers is that for equal labor time they shall, when the values of the invested constant elements have been deducted, receive equal values, whereas the difference in the rates of profit is a matter of no moment to them, just as the modern wage earner is indifferent as to what rate of profit the quantum of surplus value extorted out of him may represent.

But the comparison is fallacious. For, says Böhm-Bawerk, the laborers of our day do not receive the surplus value, whereas in the supposed case the two laborers do receive it. It is therefore not an indifferent matter whether it be allotted to them by one measure or by another, by the measure of the work done or by the measure of the invested means of production. Consequently the inequality in the rates of profit cannot depend on the fact that the magnitude of the rate of profit is of no moment to the persons concerned.

These last sentences are a salient example of Böhm-Bawerk's polemic method. He completely ignores his opponent's actual line of argument, and quotes an illustrative example (which he proceeds to interpret falsely) as if it had been alleged to be a proof; he then triumphantly announces that an example is not a proof. The difference with which we have to do is the difference between pre-capitalist and capitalist competition. In the local market which it dominates, pre-capitalist competition effectuates the equalization of the different individual values to produce a single market value; capitalist competition effectuates the transformation of value into price of production. This, however, is only possible because capital and labor can remove at will from one sphere of production to another; this removal cannot take place freely until all legal and material obstacles to the transfer have ceased to exist, cannot take place until (disregarding minor considerations) there exists absolute liberty of movement for capital and for labor. But in pre-capitalist conditions this *competition for spheres of investment* is impossible, and consequently the equalization of the different rates of profit is impossible. Since this is so, since the laborer who produces on his own account cannot change his sphere of production at will, the difference in the profit rates conjoined with equal masses of profit (= surplus value), is indifferent to him, just as to the wage laborer it is of no moment what rate of profit is represented by the amount of surplus value extorted from him. The *tertium comparationis* [the third term in the comparison] is in both cases that the laborers' chief concern is with the amount of surplus value. For whether they get the surplus value or not, in both cases they have to do the work which produces it. It depends strictly upon the duration of their labor. The matter may be expressed in arithmetical terms as follows. Let us suppose that there are two producers each of whom works on his own account, that one of them makes use of means of

51

production amounting to 10 shillings daily, and that the other makes use of means of production amounting to 20 shillings daily. Let us further suppose that each of them daily produces new value to the amount of 20 shillings. The first laborer will receive 40 shillings for his product, the second will receive 30 shillings; of the 40 shillings 20, and of the 30 shillings 10, will be reconverted into means of production, so that there will remain for each laborer 20 shillings. Since they are not free to change the sphere of production at will, the inequality of the rates of profit is of no consequence to them. Of the 20 shillings which remain at the disposal of each, let 10 shillings represent the portion used to provide the laborer's means of subsistence, or (in capitalist phraseology) let 10 shillings represent their variable capital, then for each of them the remaining 10 shillings will constitute surplus value. For a modern capitalist the affair would assume a very different complexion. In the first sphere he would have to disburse capital amounting to 30 shillings in the form of $20c = 10v$ in order to gain 10 shillings surplus value; in the second sphere, if he invested an equal amount of capital, it would be in the form of $15c + 15v$ and he would gain 15 shillings surplus value in return for his outlay. Since capital is transferable at will there will be competition between the investments until the profits are equalized, which will ensue when the prices are no longer 40 shillings and 30 shillings respectively, but 35 shillings in each case.

But Böhm-Bawerk's polemic secures its triumph in the "arithmetical exposition" of the example given by Marx. In this exposition the simple production of commodities presupposed by Marx is in the twinkling of an eye transformed into capitalist production. For with what else than capitalist production have we to do when Böhm-Bawerk equips one of the laborers with means of production requiring five years to furnish, while the means of production required by the other laborer can be furnished in a time measured in days? Does not this imply differences in the organic composition of capital, differences which, when so extensive, can arise only as the outcome of capitalist development? In the case of the laborer who works on his own account, such a laborer as Marx had in view, the means of production are tools of a comparatively simple kind, and there is no very notable difference in value between the tools used in the different spheres of production. Where tools of considerable value are employed (a fulling mill, for instance) these are usually the property of the guild or of the city, and each guildsman's share therein is insignificant. Speaking generally, in pre-capitalist conditions dead labor plays a modest part as compared with living labor. Although, however, the differences in question are inconsiderable, they do in fact suffice to determine certain differences in the rates of profit, differences whose equalization is hindered by the artificial barriers surrounding every sphere of production. But wherever the means of production bulked largely in comparison with labor, co-operative industry made its appearance at an early date, was speedily transformed into capitalist industry, and as a rule culminated in legalized or virtual monopoly (as in the mining industry).

Marx further assumes that the laborers in his illustration mutually exchange their respective products. Böhm-Bawerk complains of the injustice involved, in that one of the laborers, after working for six years, should receive merely an equivalent for his labor time, and not be allotted in addition some compensation for the time he has had to wait. But if one of them has had to wait six years for the return, the other has had to wait six years for the product, has had to store up his own products for six years that he may be able at last to exchange them for the former's product, now at length completed. Hence there is no occasion for allotting a special compensation to one of the two. But in reality there is no more historical warrant for the assumption of so great a divergence between the times when returns can be expected, than there is for the similar assumption of an extensive variation in the organic composition of the "capital."

Böhm-Bawerk, however, is not content with the Middle

Ages. In the "modern world," too, relationships exist which correspond to those of the Marxist hypothesis. They are found, says our critic, as Marx himself indicates, in the case of the land-owning peasant farmer and of the handicraftsman. These ought to secure equal incomes whether the capital they have invested in means of production amounts to Io shillings or to 10,000 shillings, a supposition which manifestly conflicts with the facts. Certainly it conflicts with the facts. But Marx never maintained that in the "modern" world two distinct prices obtain for an article according as it has been produced by capitalists or by handicraftsmen. As far as the "modern" world is concerned, Marx is referring, not to capitalist conditions, but to the medieval system as contrasted with the classical. This is manifest from the context, and it seems almost incredible that Böhm-Bawerk should have misunderstood the passage as he has done.

However, Böhm-Bawerk assures us that Marx's views as to the equalization of the rates of profit are historically untenable, and refers in this connection to an objection raised by Werner Sombart in the latter's criticism of Marx's third volume. But in actual fact Sombart makes no reference to the question of the validity of the law of value in pre-capitalist conditions. All he does is to oppose the contention that during the transition from the medieval to the capitalist economy, the equalization of the rates of profit has been brought about by the leveling of the originally unequal rates of surplus value. He holds, rather, that the starting point of capitalist competition is from the very outset to be found in the pre-existing commercial rate of profit. Had surplus value been the starting point, capitalism would first have seized upon the spheres in which living labor predominated, and only gradually would it have proceeded to exploit other spheres of production, in proportion as in those spheres prices had fallen owing to a great increase in production. In truth production develops with especial vigor in spheres wherein there is much constant capital, as for example in the mining industry. Capital would have had no reason to transfer itself from one sphere of production to another without a prospect of a "customary profit" such as existed in commercial profit. But, continues Sombart, the error can be shown in yet another way. If, at the outset of capitalist production, exorbitant profits had been obtainable in spheres where variable capital preponderated, this would imply that all at once capital had made use as wage earners of those who had hitherto been independent producers, had employed them at half the amount which they had previously earned for themselves, and had pocketed all the difference realizable by the sale of the commodities at prices corresponding to their values. In actual fact, says Sombart, capitalist production began with the exploitation of declassed individuals, and in spheres of production some of which were completely new creations; unquestionably, therefore, capitalist production started from the fixing of prices directly in relation to the amount of capital invested. [6]

In opposition to Sombart, my own opinion is that equalization of the different rates of surplus value to form a single rate of profit was the outcome of a process long drawn out. In Sombart's opinion it would be incomprehensible that the capitalist should have troubled to gain control of production unless he had a prospect of securing as industrial capitalist the same profit which he had been in the habit of securing as a merchant. It seems to me, however, that Sombart overlooks the consideration that the merchant did not in the first instance cease to be a merchant when he became a manufacturer. The capital he employed in export was still his main concern. But by employing his extra capital (and in view of the comparatively small amount of constant capital then requisite, no considerable sum would be needed) for the production of commodities on his own account, he was enabled to provide the necessary articles more regularly and in larger quantities–important considerations in a rapidly expanding market. In the second place, inasmuch as he appropriated part of the surplus value produced by the handicraftsmen he transferred to the new industry, he realized an extra profit. Even if the profit rate he could secure on the capital invested in industry was lower than that obtainable on his commercial capital, nevertheless the total rate of profit was henceforth greater. However, a rapid increase in his industrial profit rate occurred when, through the utilization of new technical methods (the association of labor, and factory production), he was enabled to produce articles more cheaply than his competitors, who were still satisfying their demand with commodities produced by independent handicraftsmen. Competition then forced his rivals to adopt the new method of production and to disregard the products of the handicraftsmen's labor. With the further progress of capitalism, when production no longer took place mainly for the purposes of the mercantile exporter, and when the capitalist began to effect a conquest of the whole market, his profit was chiefly dependent upon the following factors: His technical methods of production were superior, so that he could produce more cheaply than the handicraftsmen. Since for the time being the market value of the handicraftsman's products determined prices, the capitalist was able to realize extra surplus value or extra profit, which was greater in proportion as his technical superiority was more marked. For the most part, through special legal privileges, the exploitation of superior technical methods was a monopoly of individual capitalists. Not until the days of monopoly were over, not until the restrictions upon the transferability of capital had been abolished, not until the shackles of the laborer had been removed, was the equalization of the varying rates of profit, originally so divergent, rendered possible.

First of all, by the supplanting of handicraftsmanship and by the increase of competition within the sphere of capitalist production, the extra profit realizable by capital was reduced; and subsequently freedom of transference from one sphere of production to another effectuated the equalization of profit to become average profit.

The expansion of the market creates a need for enhanced and more regular supply, and this in turn impels commercial capital to acquire control of production as well. The profit which capital thus realizes may be less than commercial profit. For to capital it assumes the form of extra profit, which is made because the commodities which capital produces are obtainable by it more cheaply than those purchasable from independent handicraftsmen. In the further course of economic evolution, the extra profit made with the aid of superior technical equipment by the capitalist who is competing with the handicraftsman for the home market becomes the motive force for the exclusive seizure of a sphere of production by capital. The organic composition of capital plays here a minor part; and in any case, as far as precapitalist conditions are concerned, Böhm-Bawerk and Sombart overestimate the extent of differences in the organic composition of capital.

Only where, as a matter of actual fact, the means of production bulk large in importance, as is the case in the mining industry, does the great preponderance of constant capital become a reason for capitalization, for which co-operation constitutes a preliminary stage. For the most part such industries are likewise monopolies, the yield of which has to be dealt with by special laws.

As soon, however, as capitalist competition has definitively established the equal rate of profit, that rate becomes the starting point for the calculations of the capitalists in the investment of capital in newly-created branches of production. The prices here fluctuate on either side of that price of production whose attainment makes the particular branch of production appear profitable. At the same time, the capitalist goes halfway to meet competition, for he himself accepts average profit as a regulative principle, and the sole effect of competition is to prevent his deviating from the norm and from securing an above-average profit for any considerable period. It is obvious, moreover, that the formation of price in capitalist society must differ from the formation of price in social conditions based upon the simple production of commodities. We shall now pursue our examination of the

57

change in the character of the formation of price by considering the "fourth argument." Böhm-Bawerk tells us that, according to Marx, in a complex economic system the law of value regulates the prices of production, at least indirectly and in the last resort, since the total value of the commodities determined by the law of value determines the total surplus value, while this last regulates the amount of the average profit and therefore the general rate of profit (III, 211-212). The average profit determines the price of production. In the sense of the Marxist doctrine, says Böhm-Bawerk, this is correct, but the statement is incomplete, and our critic attempts to "complete" it as follows: The price of production is equal to cost price plus average profit. The cost price of the means of production consists, again, of two components: first the outlay on wages; and secondly the outlay upon means of production whose values have already been transformed into prices of production. If we continue this analysis we come at last—as does Adam Smith in his "natural price," with which, indeed, Marx expressly identifies his price of production—to resolve the price of production into two components or determinants [!]: (I) the sum total of the wages paid during the different stages of production, which taken together represent the actual cost price of the commodities; (2) the sum total of the profits calculated on all these disbursements upon wages. Consequently one determinant of the price of a commodity is the average profit incidental to its production. Of the other determinant, the wages paid, Marx speaks no further in this passage. But it is evident, says Böhm-Bawerk, that the total expended outlay upon wages is a product of the quantity of labor employed, multiplied by the average rate of wages. Since, however, according to the law of value the exchange relations must be determined solely by the *quantity* of labor expended, and since Marx denies that the rate of wages has any influence upon the value of the commodities, it is also evident that, of the two components of the factor "outlay upon wages," only the amount of labor expended is in harmony with the law of value, while in the second component, rate of wages, a determinant alien to the law of value enters among the determinants of the prices of production.

It is almost incredible, the way in which Böhm-Bawerk deduces as a self-evident inference from Marx's train of thought the very conclusion which Marx has in so many words stigmatized as a gross fallacy. Let Marx speak for himself. "The value of the annual product in commodities, just like the value of the commodities produced by some particular investment of capital, and like the value of any individual commodity, resolves itself into two parts: Part A, which replaces the value of the advanced constant capital, and Part B, which presents itself in the form of revenue as wages, profit, and rent. This last part of value, B, stands in opposition to Part A to the extent that this Part A, under otherwise equal circumstances, in the first place never assumes the form of revenue, and in the second place always flows back in the form of capital, and of constant capital at that. The other portion, B, however, carries within itself an antagonism. Profit and rent have this in common with wages that all three of them are forms of revenue. Nevertheless, they differ essentially from each other in that profit and rent are surplus value, unpaid labor, whereas wages are paid labor." [7]

In that he reproduces as Marx's opinion "the incredible error in analysis which permeates the whole of political economy since Adam Smith," Böhm-Bawerk makes a double mistake. First of all he ignores constant capital. Apart from all else, this is least permissible in a place in which we have to do with the transformation of value into price of production. For what is decisive for this transformation is the organic composition of the capital, that is to say, the ratio between the constant and the variable capital. To disregard the constant capital in this case is to disregard the most essential point, is to render it quite impossible to understand the formation of the price of production. But graver, perhaps, is the second mistake. Inasmuch as Böhm-Bawerk, in common with Adam Smith, makes variable capital and surplus value "component parts," or as he puts it more stringently, "determinants," of value, he perverts Marx's doctrine into its precise opposite. For Marx, value is the *prius,* the thing given, while v and s are no more than parts whose magnitude is limited by the new value added to the dead labor (c) and determined in accordance with the quantity of labor. How much of this new value (which can be resolved into v + s, but does not originate from them) can be assigned to v and how much to s, is determined by the value of the labor power, which is equal to the value of the means of subsistence necessary for its maintenance, the balance remaining available for surplus value. Böhm-Bawerk is still entangled in the capitalist illusion in accordance with which the cost price is regarded as a constitutive factor of the value or of the price. Precisely because he ignores c, he makes it utterly impossible for himself to gain insight into the process of the formation of value. He does not see that in the product the portion of the cost price which represents the constant capital appears reproduced with its value unchanged. It is otherwise with the portion represented by v. The value of the variable capital presents itself in the form of the means of subsistence consumed by the laborer. The value of these means of subsistence is annihilated in the process of consumption. But the new value produced by the laborers belongs to the capitalist; a portion of this new value is re-invested by him in variable capital, and seems to him to replace this again and again, just as another portion of the value which flows back to him replaces the constant capital whose value is actually transferred to the product. The distinction between c and v is thereby obliterated, and the process of the formation of value is enveloped in mystery. Labor no longer manifests itself as the source of value, for value appears to be constituted out of the cost price plus an excess over cost price coming no matter whence. Thus the "price of labor" seems to be the cause of the price of the product, so that ultimately the whole analysis resolves itself into the circular explanation of price by price. Instead of conceiving of value as a magnitude which, in accordance with definite laws, undergoes subdivison into two portions, one of which replaces the constant capital, while the other becomes revenue (v + s), revenue itself is made a constituent of price, and the constant capital is forgotten. Thus, Marx expressly insists that "it would be a mistake to say that the value of wages, the rate of profit, and the rate of rent form independent constituent elements of value, whose composition gives rise to the value of commodities, leaving aside the constant part; in other words, it mould be a mistake to say that they are constituent elements of the value of commodities, or of the price of production" (III, 994).

If, however, the wage of labor be not a constituent of value, it naturally has no influence upon the magnitude of value. How, then, is it possible for Böhm-Bawerk to continue to proclaim that it has an influence upon value? To demonstrate this influence, he gives us two tables. Three commodities, A, B, and C, have at the outset the same price of production, namely 100, while the organic composition of the capital differs in each case. The daily wage is 5; the rate of surplus value (s') is 100 percent; the total capital being 1,500, the average rate of profit (p) is 10 percent.

Commodity	Working Days	Wages	Capital Employed	Average Profit	Price of Production
A	10	50	500	50	100
B	6	30	700	70	100
C	14	70	300	30	100
Totals	30	150	1,500	150	300

Now let us assume that wages rise from 5 to 6; of the 300, 180 will now accrue to wages and 120 to profit; p' is now 8 percent; the table, therefore, must be modified as follows:

Commodity	Working Days	Wages	Capital Employed	Average Profit	Price of Production
A	10	60	500	40	100
B	6	36	700	56	92
C	14	84	300	24	108
Totals	30	180	1,500	120	300

The tables exhibit certain peculiarities. Namely, we are not told the magnitude of the constant capital employed in the various branches, nor do we learn how much of the constant capital is transferred to the product; thus only is Böhm-Bawerk enabled to draw the conclusion that although a notable constant capital is employed, it nowhere reappears in the product, and the prices of production are identical. Still less are we able to understand how it happens that higher wages can be paid with the same capital. It is true that these errors make little difference to the final results, for Böhm-Bawerk does in a sense allow for the organic composition, inasmuch as he calculates the profit upon varying outlays of capital; and his second survey alters only the absolute figures, not the relative ones, for the rate of profit undergoes a greater fall than Böhm-Bawerk declares, seeing that the total capital is increased. But the failure to take the constant capital into account renders it impossible to secure an insight into the actual process. If we correct Böhm-Bawerk's tables, they read as follows:

Commodity	Total Capital $c + v$	c	v	s	p	Value	Price of Production
A	500	450	50	50	50	550	550
B	700	670	30	30	70	730	770
C	300	230	70	70	30	370	330
Totals	1,500	1,350	150	150	150	1,650	1,650 = 1,500 + 150

To avoid complicating the calculation needlessly, we have assumed that c is entirely used up. If the wage now rises from 5 to 6, the total capital is increased from 1,500 to 1,530, because v increases from 150 to 180; the surplus value is reduced to 120, the rate of surplus value to 66.6 percent, and the rate of profit to approximately 7.8 percent. The new value created by the laborers remains unchanged, and is 300. But the organic composition of the capital has been modified, and therewith has been modified the factor that is decisive in the transformation of value into price of production.

Commodity	Total Capital c + v	c	v	s	p	Value	Price of Production
A	510	450	60	40	40	550	550
B	706	670	36	24	55	730	761
C	314	230	84	56	25	370	339
Totals	1,530	1,350	180	120	120	1,650	1,650

The table shows the "effects of general fluctuations of wages on prices of production" (III, Chap. XI). We obtain the following laws [8] : (I) as far as a capital of average composition is concerned, the price of production of the commodities undergoes no change; (2) as far as a capital of lower composition is concerned, the price of production of the commodities rises, but not proportionally to the fall in the profits; (3) as far as a capital of higher composition is concerned, the price of production falls, but not as much as the profit (III, 236). What are we to deduce from this? If we are to believe Böhm-Bawerk, it appears that a rise in wages (the quantity of labor remaining unchanged) brings about a material alteration in the originally equal prices of production. This alteration can be ascribed in part only to the change in the rate of profit. Not wholly, of course, seeing that, for example, the price of production of commodity C has risen notwithstanding the fall in the rate of profit. This puts it beyond doubt that in the magnitude of wages we have to do with a price-determinant whose efficacy is not exhausted in the influencing of the magnitude of the profit, but which rather exercises *a direct influence of its own.* Böhm-Bawerk therefore believes that he has good reason for undertaking an independent examination of this link in the chain of determinants of price which Marx has passed over. (Marx has a special chapter on the subject!)

We have already seen that this "independence" is pushed so far as to represent Marx as saying the opposite of what he really thought. We now see how far Böhm-Bawerk's independence transcends the rules of logic. The same change in wages effects in the first case no change in the price, in the second case it causes a rise, and in the third case it causes a fall in the price. And this is what he calls having "a direct influence of its own" on price! In fact, however, the tables show clearly that wages can neither constitute components nor determinants of price; for, were it otherwise, an increase in these components must raise price and a decrease in these components must lower price. Nor can average profit constitute a magnitude independently influencing price, for if such an influence existed, whenever the profit falls the price must also fall. But by ignoring the constant portion of capital, and by thus leaving out of consideration the organic composition of capital, Böhm-Bawerk deprives himself of the possibility of explaining the process.

Speaking generally, we cannot gain an insight into the entire process from the standpoint of the individual capital, but this is the outlook to which we are restricted when we conceive the wage of labor to be an independent component of price. From this outlook it is impossible to understand how the capitalist can fail to be indemnified in the price for an increase in wages, for a greater outlay of capital. Nothing but the social relationships whose essence is disclosed by the law of value suffices to explain how the same cause, an increase in wages, can exercise so divergent an effect upon the individual capitals, the effect varying as the ratio varies in which they respectively participate in the *surplus-value-creating process of the social capital*. Their participation in the social surplus-value-creating process is, however, indicated by their organic composition.

But the changed relationship between the capitals consists in this, that their share in the production of the total surplus value has been altered; the surplus value has diminished; but the respective capitals have contributed in varying manners to this diminution, according to variations in the magnitude of the labor they have respectively set in motion. Since, however, the reduced surplus value is to be distributed among them in like manner, the modification of their respective parts in the production of surplus value must find expression in a modification of the prices. The capitals, therefore, must not be regarded individually, as Böhm-Bawerk regards them, but must be apprehended in their social interconnections, as parts, that is to say, of social capital. But the part they respectively play in the creation of the total value of the social product is only to be recognized by a knowledge of their organic composition, by a knowledge of the relationship in which the dead labor, whose value is merely transferred, stands to the living labor which creates new value and of which the variable capital is the index. To disregard this organic composition is tantamount to disregarding the social relationships of the individual capital. This renders it equally impossible to understand the process whereby value is transformed into price of production, and to understand the laws which regulate variations in the price of production–laws different from those which regulate variations in value, but always traceable in the ultimate analysis to variations in the relationships of value.

"Seeing that the price of production in the second illustration rises, while it falls in the third, it is evident from these opposite effects brought about by a fall in the rate of surplus value or by a general rise of wages that there is no prospect of any compensation in the price for the rise in wages, since the fall of the price of production in III cannot very well compensate the capitalist for the fall in the profit, and since the rise of the price in II does not prevent a fall in profit. On the contrary, in either case, whether the price rises or falls, the profit remains the same as that of the average capital whose price remains unchanged.....It follows from this, that if the price did not rise in II and fall in III, II would have to sell below and III above the new, recently reduced, average profit. It is quite evident that a rise of wages must affect a capitalist who has invested one tenth of his capital in wages differently from one who has invested one fourth or one half, according to whether 50, 25, or 10 percent of capital are advanced for wages. An increase in the price of production on one side, and a fall on the other, according to whether a capital is below or above the average social composition, is effected only by leveling to the new reduced average profit. It is clear that when, in consequence of the establishment of a general rate of profit for the capitals of lower composition (those wherein v is above the average), the values are lowered on the occasion of their transformation into prices of production, for the capitals of higher composition the values will be increased." [9] The variation in the price of production consequent upon a change in wages manifests itself as a direct effect of the new average rate of profit. As we have previously seen, the establishment of this rate is an outcome of capitalist competition. Böhm-Bawerk's polemic is therefore primarily unfortunate in this, that it is not directed against the decisive point, but against a phenomenon which only makes its appearance as a necessary consequence, as a sequel, of the primary condition, which is the formation of the price of production upon the basis of the equal rate of profit.

It makes no difference to the regulation of the price of production by the law of value, that in the wage of labor itself, that is to say in the magnitude of the variable portion of capital which has to be advanced, the transformation of the values of the laborer's necessary means of subsistence into prices of production has already been completed. We must not attempt to prove the contention that the price of production of a commodity is not regulated by the law of value, by maintaining the same thing of another commodity, to wit, labor power. For the deviation of the variable portion of capital takes place according to exactly the same laws as are observed in the case of any other commodity; in this respect there is no difference between the variable and the constant portion of capital. Only because Böhm-Bawerk makes the "value of the labor power" a determinant of the value of the product, does he fall into the error of looking upon the deviation in the price of labor power from its value as a disturbance of the law of value. Again, the magnitude of the total surplus value is unaffected by this deviation. For the total surplus value, which is equal to the total profit and regulates the rate of profit, is calculated for the social capital, where the deviations of the prices of production from value balance each other.

One more only of Böhm-Bawerk's objections remains to be considered. Even if, as Marx declares, the total surplus value regulates the average rate of profit, this nevertheless constitutes but one determinant, while as a second determinant, completely independent of the first, and *likewise completely independent of the law of value,* there operates the magnitude of the capital existing in society. Now, apart from the fact that the magnitude of the social capital is here assumed by Böhm-Bawerk to be known (which presupposes the law of value, since we have to do with the determination of the magnitude of a value), the objection has been expressly refuted by Marx, who writes: "The proportion of the sum of appropriated surplus values to the advanced total capital of society varies. Since the variation in this case is not due to the rate of surplus value, it must be due to the total capital, or rather to its constant part. The mass of this part, technically speaking, increases or decreases in proportion to the quantity of labor power bought by the variable capital, and the mass of its value increases or decreases with the increase or decrease of its own mass. Its mass of value, then, increases or decreases likewise in proportion to the mass of the value of the variable capital. If the same labor sets more constant capital in motion, labor has become more productive. If less, less productive. There has then been a change in the productivity of labor, and a change must have taken place in the value of certain commodities. The following rule then applies.

67

If the price of production of a certain commodity changes in consequence of a change in the average rate of profit, its own value may have remained unchanged, but a change must have taken place in the value of other commodities" (III, 240).

Footnotes

1. Vol III, p. 206

2. Vol III, p. 182

3. Above, pp. 29 ff.

4. Above, pp. 32 ff.

5. See Friedrich Engels, "Erganzung und Nachtrag zum dritten Buch des 'Kapital,'" *Die Neue Zeit,* Vol. I, p. 7. [Reprinted in *Engels on Capital* (1937), p. 97.]

6. Sombart, op. cit., p. 585.

7. Vol. III, p. 977.

8. Rise in wages is alone considered. Naturally a fall in wages would have the contrary effect.

9. Vol. III, p. 237.

Chapter III
The Subjectivist Outlook

THE phenomenon of variations in the price of production has shown us that the phenomena of capitalist society can never be understood if the commodity or capital be considered in isolation. It is the social relationship which these occupy, and changes in that relationship, which control and elucidate the movements of individual capitals, themselves no more than portions of the total social capital. But the representative of the psychological school of political economy fails to see this social nexus, and he therefore necessarily misunderstands a theory which definitely aims at disclosing the social determinism of economic phenomena, a theory whose starting point therefore is society and not the individual. In apprehending and expounding this theory he is ever influenced by his own individualistic mentality, and he thus arrives at contradictions which he ascribes to the theory, while they are in truth ascribable solely to his interpretations of the theory.

This confusion may be traced in all the stages of Böhm-Bawerk's polemic. Even the fundamental concept of the Marxist system, the concept of value-creating labor, is apprehended in a purely subjective manner. To him "labor" is identical with "trouble" or "effort" ["Mühe"].To make this individual feeling of distaste the cause of value naturally leads us to see in value a purely psychological fact, and to deduce the value of commodities from our *evaluation of the labor* they have cost. As is well known, this is the foundation which Adam Smith adopts for his theory of value, for he is ever inclined to abandon the objective standpoint for a subjective. Smith writes: "Equal quantities of labor must at all times and places be of equal value to the laborer. In his ordinary state of health, strength, and spirits; in the ordinary degree of his skill and dexterity, he must always lay down the same portion of his ease, his liberty, and his happiness." [1] If labor regarded as "trouble" be the basis of our personal estimate of value, then the "value of the labor" is a constituent, or a "determinant" as Böhm-Bawerk puts it, of the value of commodities. But it need not be the only one, for a number of other factors which influence the subjective estimates made by individuals take their places beside labor and have an equal right to be regarded as determinants of value. If, therefore, we identify the value of commodities with the personal estimate of the value of these commodities made by this or that individual, it seems quite arbitrary to select labor as the sole basis for such an estimate.

From the subjectivist standpoint, therefore, the standpoint from which Böhm-Bawerk levels his criticism, the labor theory of value appears untenable from the very outset. And it is because he adopts this standpoint that Böhm-Bawerk is unable to perceive that Marx's concept of labor is totally opposed to his own. Already in *A Contribution to the Critique of Political Economy* Marx had emphasized his opposition to Adam Smith's subjectivist outlook by writing "[Smith] fails to see the objective equalization of different kinds of labor which the social process forcibly carries out, mistaking it for the subjective equality of the labors of individuals." [2] In truth, Marx is entirely unconcerned with the individual motivation of the estimate of value. In capitalist society it would be absurd to make "trouble" the measure of value, for speaking generally the owners of the products have taken no trouble at all, whereas the trouble has been taken by those who have produced but do not own them. With Marx, in fact, every individual relationship is excluded from the conception of value-creating labor; labor is regarded, not as something which arouses feelings of pleasure or its opposite, but as an objective magnitude, inherent in the commodities, and determined by the degree of development of social productivity. Whereas for Böhm-Bawerk, labor seems merely one of the determinants in personal estimates of value, in Marx's view labor is the basis and connective tissue of human society, and in Marx's view the degree of productivity of labor

70

and the method of organization of labor determine the character of social life. Since labor, viewed in its social function as the total labor of society of which each individual labor forms merely an aliquot part, is made the principle of value, economic phenomena are subordinated to objective laws independent of the individual will and controlled by social relationships. Beneath the husk of economic categories we discover social relationships, relationships of production, wherein commodities play the part of intermediaries, the social relationships being reproduced by these intermediate processes, or undergoing a gradual transformation until they demand a new type of inter-mediation.

Thus the law of value becomes a law of motion for a definite type of social organization based upon the production of commodities, for in the last resort all change in social structure can be referred to changes in the relationships of production, that is to say to changes in the evolution of productive power and in the organization of [productive] labor. We are thereby led, in the most striking contrast to the outlook of the psychological school, to regard political economy as a part of sociology, and sociology itself as a historical science. Böhm-Bawerk has never become aware of this contrast of outlooks. The question whether the "subjectivist method" or the "objectivist method" is the sound method in economics he decides in a controversy with Sombart by saying that each method must supplement the other—whereas in truth we are not concerned at all with two different methods, but with contrasted and mutually exclusive outlooks upon the whole of social life. Thus it happens that Böhm-Bawerk, unfailingly carrying on the controversy from his subjectivist and psychological standpoint, discovers contradictions in the Marxist theory which seem to him to be contradictions solely because of his own subjectivist interpretation of the theory.

But if labor be the only measure for the estimate of value and therewith the only measure of value, it is as regards this subjectivist outlook only logical that in that case commodities should exchange solely by the measure of equal quantities of labor embodied in them, for otherwise it would be impossible to see what should induce the individuals to deviate from their personal estimates of value. If, however, the facts do not conform to these premises, then the law of value loses all significance, even if labor be no more than one determinant among several. This is why Böhm-Bawerk lays so much stress upon the contention that commodities are *not* exchanged one for another by the measure of equal quantities of labor. This necessarily appears to be a contradiction when value is conceived, not as an objective quantity, but as the outcome of individual motivation. For if labor be the measure for my personal estimate of value, then I shall not be inclined to exchange my good for another unless in that other I obtain something which, if I had to produce it for myself, would cost me at least as much labor as my own good has cost me. A permanent deviation of the exchange relationship is in fact, if the subjectivist conception of the law of value be once assumed, a contradiction per se, a suspension of the meaning (that is to say, of the subjectivist meaning) of the law of value, which here supplies the individual's motive for economic action.

Very different is Marx's outlook. In his view, that goods contain labor is one of their intrinsic qualities; that they are exchangeable is a distinct quality, one solely dependent on the will of the possessor, and one which presupposes that they are owned and alienable. The relationship of the quantity of labor to the process of exchange does not come into consideration until they are regularly *produced* as commodities, produced that is to say as goods specifically destined for exchange; thus this relationship makes its appearance only in a definite phase of historic evolution. The quantitative ratio wherein they are now exchanged becomes thereby dependent upon the time of production, which is in its turn determined by the degree of social productivity. The exchange relationship thus loses its chance character, thus ceases to be dependent upon the caprice of the owner. The social conditions imposed upon labor become objective limitations for the individual, and the social complex controls the individual's activities.

Now the mode of the social process of production determines the social process of distribution, for this latter is no longer consciously regulated, as if in a communist community. Under capitalism the process of distribution manifests itself as the outcome of the exchanges effected by independent individual producers, exchanges controlled by the laws of competition.

The Marxist law of value starts from this, that commodities exchange at their values, this meaning that commodities exchange one for another when they embody equal quantities of labor. The equality of the quantities of labor is solely a condition for the exchange of commodities at their values. Böhm-Bawerk, entangled in his subjectivist interpretation, mistakes this condition for a condition of exchange in general. But it is obvious that the exchange of commodities at their values, while on the one hand it merely constitutes the theoretical starting point for a subsequent analysis, on the other hand directly controls a historic phase of the production of commodities, a phase to which a specific kind of competition corresponds.

But the exchange relationship of commodities is no more than the material expression of the social relationships of persons, and what in fact secures realization in the exchange relationship is the *equality of the agents of production.* Because, in the simple production of commodities, equal and independent laborers severally possessed of their means of production confront one another, exchange takes place at prices which tend to correspond to the values. Thus only can the mechanism of the simple production of commodities be maintained; thus only can the conditions requisite for the reproduction of the relationships of production be fulfilled.

In such a society the product of labor belongs to the laborer. If by permanent deviation from this rule (chance deviations are mutually compensatory) a portion of the product of labor be taken away from the laborer and assigned to another person, the foundations of the society will be modified; the former will become a wage laborer (engaged in home industry), and the latter will become a capitalist. This is actually one of the ways in which the simple production of commodities comes to an end. But it cannot come to an end unless there has occurred a modification in social relationships, carrying with it a modification in exchange, the expression of social relationships.

In the capitalist process of exchange, whose purpose is the realization of surplus value, the equality of the economic units is once more reflected. These, however, are no longer independently working producers, but owners of capital. Their equality secures expression in that the exchange is only normal when the profits are equal, when both are average profit. The exchange which gives expression to the equality of the owners of capital is of course differently determined from the exchange that is based upon an equality in the expenditure of the labor. But just as both societies have the same foundations, the division of property and the division of labor; just as capitalist society can be conceived as merely a higher modification of the earlier type of society; so also is the law of value unchanged in its foundation, for it has merely undergone certain modifications in its realization. These are caused by the specific mode of capitalist competition, which effectuates the proportional equality of capital. The share in the total product, whose value remains directly determined by the law of value, was formerly proportional to the individual's expenditure of labor, but now becomes proportional to the expenditure of capital requisite to set labor in motion. Thus the subordination of labor to capital finds expression. It appears as social subordination, the whole society being subdivided into capitalists and laborers, the former being owners of the product of the latter, the total product, determined by the law of value, being divided among the capitalists. The capitalists are free and equal; their equality is displayed in the price of production $= k + p$, where p is proportional to k. The dependent position of the laborer is shown by his appearance as one of the constituents of k, side by side with machinery, lubricating oil, and dumb beasts; this is all he is worth to the capitalist as soon as he has left the market and has taken his place in the factory to create surplus value. For a moment only did he play his part in the market, as a free man selling his labor power. The brief glory in the market and the prolonged debasement in the factory–here we see the difference between legal equality and economic equality, between the equality demanded by the bourgeoisie and the equality demanded by the proletariat.

The capitalist mode of production (this is its historic significance, and this is why we can regard it as a preliminary stage on the way to socialist society) socializes mankind to a greater extent than did any previous mode of production, that is to say, capitalism makes the existence of the individual man dependent upon the social relationships amid which he is placed. It does so in an antagonistic form, by the establishment of the two great classes, making the performance of social labor the function of one of these classes, and enjoyment of the products of labor the function of the other.

The individual is not yet an "immediate" of society, that is, he does not yet possess a direct relationship to society, for his economic position is determined by his position as member of a class. The individual can only exist as a capitalist because his class appropriates the product of the other class, and his own share is solely determined by the total surplus value, not by the surplus value individually appropriated by him.

This significance of class gives expression to the law of value as a *social* law. To confute the theory of value it must be shown to lack confirmation in *the social domain.*

In capitalist society the individual appears as ruler or slave according as he is enrolled in one or other of the two great classes. Socialist society makes him free, inasmuch as it abolishes the antagonistic form of society, inasmuch as it consciously and directly installs socialization. No longer, then, are the interrelationships of society concealed behind enigmatic economic categories which seem to be the natural qualities of things; these interrelationships now manifest themselves as the freely willed outcome of human co-operation. Political economy then ceases to exist in the form we have hitherto known, and is replaced by a science of the "wealth of nations."

Competition is the power that effects the transformation of values into prices of production. But the competition with which we have to do here is capitalist competition. Competition is further necessary to secure a sale at prices which shall fluctuate round the value. In the simple production of commodities, on the other hand, we are concerned with the reciprocal competition of the finished commodities; it is this which equates the individual values to constitute a market value, thus objectively correcting the subjective errors of individuals. But here (in capitalist society) we have to do with the competition of capitals for different spheres of investment, a competition which establishes equal rates of profit, a competition which cannot become effective until after the abolition of the legal and material shackles which had previously been imposed upon the freedom of movement of capital and labor. Whereas the continually increasing diversity in the organic composition of capital, and the consequent greater and greater variations in the masses of surplus value directly created in the individual spheres of production, are in the first instance the outcome of capitalist evolution–this evolution in turn creates the possibility and the need for extinguishing these differences as far as capital is concerned, and for thus realizing the equality of human beings *qua* owners of capital.

We have previously seen what are the laws in accordance with which this equalization is effected. We have also seen that only upon the basis of the law of value was it possible to determine the magnitude of the total profit undergoing distribution as being equal to the total surplus value, and thus to determine the extent of the deviation of the price of production from its value. We have further seen how changes in the prices of production must always be referred to changes in value, and can only be explained with reference to such changes. All that we are interested in here is to note how, in this respect also, the subjectivist outlook hinders insight into Marx's train of thought.

For Böhm-Bawerk, competition is merely a collective name for all the psychical impulses and motives by which the parties in the market are influenced, and which thus affect the formation of prices. In relation to this view he has therefore no occasion to speak in a bad sense of the equilibrium between supply and demand, seeing that a number of wants always remain unsatisfied; for what this theory is concerned about is not the effective demand, but demand in general, so that certainly it remains enigmatical how the opinions and wishes of those who cannot buy are to influence the purchasing prices. Does not Marx destroy the validity of his objective law of value when he appeals to competition, appeals, that is to say, to these psychical impulses?

The relationship between supply and demand determines the price, but the height of the price determines the relationship between supply and demand. If the demand increases, the price rises, but if the price rises, the demand lessens, while if the price falls the demand increases. Further, if the demand increases and consequently the price rises, supply increases because production has become more lucrative. Thus price determines supply and demand, and supply and demand determine price; moreover, supply determines demand, and demand supply. In addition, all these fluctuations have a tendency to neutralize one another. If demand increases, so that price rises above its normal level, supply increases; this increase readily becomes greater than needful, and price then falls below the normal. Can we find no fixed point in all this confusion?

In Böhm-Bawerk's opinion, demand and supply

invariably balance one another, whether exchange be effected at a normal price or at an irregular one. But what is this normal price? On the basis of capitalist production the surplus-value-creating process of capital is a precondition of production. In order that the capitalist may continue to produce, he must be able to sell the commodity at a price which is equal to its cost price plus average profit. If he is unable to realize this price (the normal price of the commodity produced under capitalism), the process of reproduction is arrested, and the supply is reduced to a point at which the relationship between supply and demand renders it possible to realize this price. Thus the relationship between supply and demand ceases to be a mere matter of chance; we perceive that it is regulated by the price of production, which constitutes the center around which market prices fluctuate in directions which are perpetually opposed, so that the fluctuations compensate one another in the long run. Thus the price of production is a condition of the supply, of the reproduction, of commodities. And not of this alone. It is necessary to secure such a relationship between supply and demand that the normal price, the price of production, can be realized, for then only can the course of the capitalist mode of production continue undisturbed, then only can occur the perpetual reproduction, through the very course of the process of circulation, of the social preconditions of a mode of production whose motive force is the need of capital for the creation of surplus value.

In the long run, therefore, the relationship between supply and demand must be of such a kind that price of production (brought about independently of this relationship) may be attained which shall yield the capitalist the cost price plus the profit for the sake of which he has undertaken the production. Then we speak of the equilibrium of supply and demand.

If, on the other hand, we consider demand, we find that it is "essentially conditioned on the mutual relations of the different economic classes and their relative economic positions, that is to say, first, on the proportion of the total surplus value to the wages, and secondly, on the proportion of the various parts into which surplus value is divided (profit, interest, ground rent, taxes, etc.). And this shows once more that absolutely nothing can be explained by the relation of supply and demand, unless the basis has first been ascertained on which this relation rests" (III, 214). Thus Marx supplies the objective laws which are realized by and control the "psychical impulses" of individuals. The psychological school can attempt to elucidate but one side of the question, demand. The members of that school believe that they have explained the matter when they have classified the individual needs which manifest themselves as demand. They fail to recognize that the fact that a need exists does not convey any implication of the possibility for satisfying this need. The possibility of satisfaction does not depend upon the good will of the person feeling the need; it depends upon his economic power, upon the share of the social product of which he is able to dispose, upon the magnitude of the equivalent he is able to give for products owned by other persons.

In as much as the productive power of human society in the specific form of organization which society confers upon that productive power is for Marx the fundamental idea of political economy, Marx demonstrates economic phenomena and their modifications as they manifest themselves in conformity to law, and *causally* dominated by the modifications in productive power. In this demonstration, in accordance with the dialectic method, conceptual evolution runs parallel throughout with historical evolution, inasmuch as the development of the social power of production appears in the Marxist system, on the one side as a historical reality, and on the other side as a conceptual reflex. Moreover, this parallelism furnishes the strictest empirical proof of the accuracy of the theory. The commodity form is necessarily the starting point; the commodity form is the simplest form, and becomes the object of economic contemplation, as the object of a specific scientific contemplation. For in the commodity form there already comes into being that delusive appearance which results from the fact that the social relationships of individuals assume the aspect of material qualities of things. It is this delusively material appearance which so greatly confuses the issues of economics. The social functions of individuals masquerade as material qualities of things, just as time and space, the subjective forms of perception, masquerade as objective qualities of things. Inasmuch as Marx dispels this illusion, inasmuch as he discloses personal relationships where before him material relationships had been seen, and discloses social relationships where before him individual relationships had been seen, he succeeds in furnishing a unified and consistent explanation of the phenomena which the classical economists had been unable to elucidate. The failure of the classical economists was inevitable, for they regarded bourgeois relationships of production as natural and unalterable. Marx, having demonstrated the historic conditioning of these relationships of production, was able to take up the analysis at the point where the investigations of the classical economists had been arrested.

But the demonstration of the historic transitoriness of bourgeois relationships of production signifies the close of political economy as a *bourgeois* science and its foundation as a *proletarian* science.

No more than two ways now remained open to the bourgeois champions, if they desired to be anything more than mere apologists for whom an uncritical eclecticism would provide the crumbling pillars of their systems of harmony. They might, like the historical school in Germany, ignore theory, and endeavor to fill its place with a history of economic science, but would then be restricted, as the German historical school has been restricted even within its own chosen field, by the lack of any unified apprehension of economic happenings. The psychological school of economics has chosen the other path. The members of this school have endeavored to construct a theory of economic happenings by excluding economics itself from their purview. Instead of taking economic or social relationships as the starting point of their system, they have chosen for that starting point the *individual* relationship between men and things. They regard this relationship from the psychological outlook as one which is subject to natural and unalterable laws. They ignore the relationships of production in their social determinateness, and the idea of a law-abiding evolution of economic happenings is alien to their minds. This economic theory signifies the repudiation of economics. The last word in the rejoinder of bourgeois economics to scientific socialism is the *suicide of political economy.*

Footnotes

1. *Wealth of Nations,* Book I, Chap. 5.

2. Kerr ed., p. 68.

www.ingramcontent.com/pod-product-compliance
Lightning Source LLC
Chambersburg PA
CBHW060202290526
45789CB00003B/1121